Quilting More Memories

CREATING PROJECTS WITH IMAGE TRANSFERS

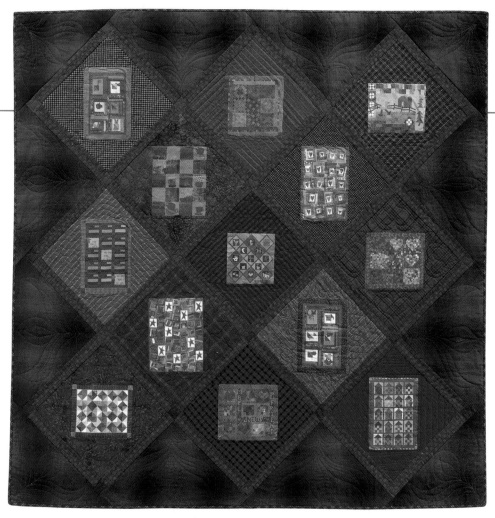

Sandy Bonsib

Martingale
& COMPANY

Bothell, Washington

Credits

President . . . . Nancy J. Martin
CEO . . . . Daniel J. Martin
Publisher . . . . Jane Hamada
Editorial Director . . . . Mary V. Green
Editorial Project Manager . . . . Tina Cook
Design and Production Manager . . . . Stan Green
Technical Editor . . . . Ursula Reikes
Copy Editor . . . . Lily G. Casura
Illustrator . . . . Laurel Strand
Photographer . . . . Brent Kane
Cover and Text Designer . . . . Jennifer LaRock Shontz

That Patchwork Place is an imprint of Martingale & Co.

Quilting More Memories: Creating Projects with
   Image Transfers
© 2001 by Sandy Bonsib

Martingale & Company
PO Box 118
Bothell, WA 98041-0118 USA
www.patchwork.com

Printed in Hong Kong
06 05 04 03 02 01   6 5 4 3 2 1

On the Cover: *A Quilt of My Quilts* by Sandy Bonsib

The quilt on page 4 includes images from *A Farmer's Alphabet* by Mary Azarian, Illustrations by Mary Azarian. Reprinted by permission of David R. Godine, Publisher, Inc. ©1981 by Mary Azarian, illustrations by Mary Azarian.

Mission Statement

We are dedicated to providing quality products

and service by working together to inspire

creativity and to enrich the lives we touch.

Library of Congress Cataloging-in-Publication Data

Bonsib, Sandy.
   Quilting more memories: creating projects with image transfers / Sandy Bonsib.
        p.   cm.
   ISBN 1-56477-349-3
   1. Transfer-printing. 2. Iron-on transfers.
   3. Photographs on cloth. 4. Quilting. I. Title.

TT852 .B65 2001
746.46—dc21

00-050007

Acknowledgments

Without the help of my husband, John Bickley, and my teenagers, Ben and Kate, I would never be able to write books. They help me with endless details as I work, and take over many daily chores so I can meet my deadlines. Even after more than twenty years together, I still think of John as the most kind and helpful person I know, and his support is invaluable. Ben, my resident computer genius, knows how to fix any problem I've ever had. He even bought me a laptop computer recently because it was so much faster than my old computer. I was hoping to learn to use it for this book but I didn't have time. Kate must have baked a million chocolate chip cookies to keep my students happy in the last few months. She is also my resident consultant on fabrics, settings, and border choices. Her ideas make my work easier and my quilts so much better. My family, along with our many animals, provides endless inspiration for the themes of my photo-transfer quilts.

Many thanks also go to:

Georgia Bonesteel for encouraging me to write a second book about photo transfers on fabric, for teaching photo-transfer classes to help spread the word about these very special quilts, and for sharing her students and their beautiful quilts with me, many of which I have included in this book.

Trish Carey, my mentor and dear friend. Mentors are hard to come by, and you're the best.

Sharon and Jason Yenter, owners of In the Beginning Fabrics, for having the most wonderful quilt shop I've ever seen, and for giving me so many opportunities to do what I love.

The many students around the country who have taken my classes and made such wonderful photo-transfer quilts. I have learned as much from you as you have from me.

Everyone who submitted quilts for possible publication in this book. It takes guts to submit a quilt and risk that it may not be accepted. Everyone who sent me quilts took this risk. Without your support this book would not have been possible.

Lorinda Lie, author of *Wool Quilts,* who was my "wool consultant," advising me about how to prepare wool for photo transfers.

Constance Potter Bruce, for permission to use the images from the book *Mrs. Goose Quilt,* written by her mother, Miriam Clark Potter.

Ursula Reikes, my editor for all three of my books, for her patience, understanding, expert skills, and for being a good friend as well.

And finally, to Martingale & Company for once again believing in me.

Dedication

*T*his book is dedicated to my quilt group, the Flannel Folks and Button Babes. Not only have they submitted quilts for this and my previous book about photo transfers, but they also have helped out in every possible way, from gathering materials, making blocks, sewing bindings, even calling to see how I was doing these last weeks before my deadline and offering help in many ways, time and again. Thank you—Lynn Ahlers, Pam Keller, Karen Long, Cathy Markham Mathes, Linda Petrick Nelson, Kathy Staley, Kay Stotesbery, and Sue Van Gerpen. You make my work so much fun and so much easier.

ABC for You and Me by Sandy Bonsib, 2000, Issaquah, Washington, 60" x 60". Machine quilted by Becky Kraus.
These letters, from *A Farmer's Alphabet* by Mary Azarian, remind me of the years when I was a teacher of young children. I have always loved alphabets, and these woodcuts are especially charming. I photo-transferred them, with permission, onto different tan and green wool fabrics, then appliquéd the letters onto a brown wool background with a blanket stitch and perle cotton. The folk hearts were cut from hand-dyed wool and attached with a running stitch and perle cotton. The binding is cotton homespun rather than wool, since wool would have been too bulky. I used the thinnest cotton batting I could find so that this quilt would be soft and pliable despite the heavy wool.

Contents

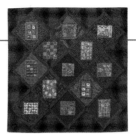

Introduction

*M*y first book on photo-transfer quilts, *Quilting Your Memories,* was published by Martingale & Company in 1999.

There are several reasons I chose to do a second, follow-up book on this exciting quilting method. For one thing, the technology is constantly changing. Transfer papers are getting better than ever. Those used in color laser copiers are more readily accepted at copy shops. Some inkjet transfer papers are now permanent and can withstand laundering. Photos can also be directly transferred to fabric. If you're trying photo transferring for the first time, it's easier than ever. And if you're making your second, third, or fourth photo-transfer quilt, you have more choices about how to transfer images to fabric.

Additionally, interest in making quilts that feature photographs continues to increase. More people want to learn this technique because the quilts that result are unique and personal. My classes, once half full, are now full—with waiting lists. There are certain questions students have asked me repeatedly as I travel and teach. I hope this book answers those questions, and more. And I hope to encourage anyone who is interested in making a photo-transfer quilt to realize that by following a few simple guidelines and choosing perhaps only one photograph, anyone with basic sewing skills can make a photo-transfer quilt that will be cherished for generations.

More people are making quilts and practicing the technique. Quilters are using different fabrics and different textures. In this book there are quilts done on 100 percent–cotton fabrics that are thicker, thinner, or

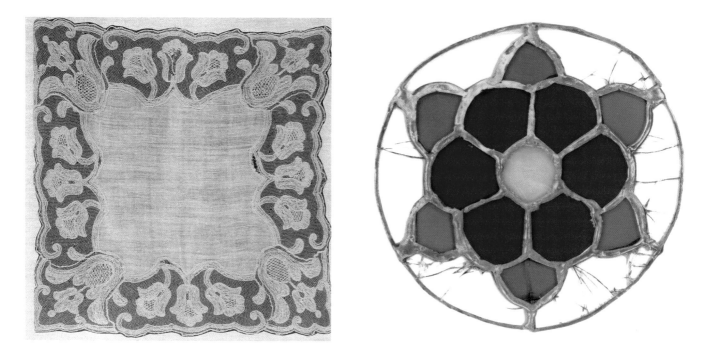

Photocopying three-dimensional objects lends dimension to image transfers.

more textured than our usual choices, as well as quilts that display photos transferred onto linen, wool, and even satin made from raw silk.

The quality of the quilts being made is getting better and better—not that great photo-transfer quilts weren't being made two or three years ago. But photo transferring has been around for a while, and the technique is constantly evolving. Quilters are transferring more than just photographs to fabric. In this book, you'll find quilts with pictures from old books (reprinted with permission, of course), leaves, and stalks of wheat. Some three-dimensional items can be photocopied just like a piece of paper. This not only eliminates the need to take a picture and get it developed, it also often results in a clearer, more colorful image. Because of the way light shadows the object as the copier "photographs" it, the resulting image has a wonderful three-dimensional look. You can even copy items like gold charms, buttons, embroidered pieces, stained glass, and Grandmother's handkerchief to create interesting photo transfers.

This book, unlike my earlier *Quilting Your Memories,* includes patterns for ten quilts that feature photo transfers. These are provided for those who prefer exact dimensions and fabric specifications. Use these quilts as a starting point to create your own special memory quilts. Refer to "Inspirational Gallery" on pages 34–55 to see how others have used photo transfers in their quilts.

Making a Photo-Transfer Quilt

*I*n this book, I'll detail every step involved in making a photo-transfer quilt, but let's start with a "big picture" introduction to the process.

1. Choose the images first. Spread your pictures on a table or floor, and then look for inspiration. Are certain photos particularly appealing? Do one or more photos suggest a theme? You don't want to start designing your quilt yet, but it's never too soon to consider the possibilities.

2. Make your photo transfers. We'll cover various fabric and transfer-method options in "Transferring Photos to Fabric" on pages 8–9.

3. Choose coordinating fabrics after you've made the transfers. It's unlikely that the colors of your transfers will exactly match the colors in your original image, so it's vital that you coordinate fabrics with transfers on fabrics rather than with the original photos. In "Choosing Coordinating Fabrics" on pages 20–22, I share tips on fabric selection.

4. Design and construct your quilt. We'll discuss the idiosyncrasies of photo-transfer design in "Getting Started" on pages 18–19, and "Designing Your Quilt" on pages 19–28.

Transferring Photos to Fabric

There are a number of ways to transfer photos or other images to fabric. The ones we'll discuss in this book are using a color copier and photo-transfer paper; using transfer paper made for an inkjet printer; and using fabric "sheets" to print the image directly onto fabric.

TIP

Practice makes perfect. As with any new technique, enthusiasm and creativity create high expectations, and invariably mistakes will happen. With photo transfers, you may be learning several new techniques, or you may be using familiar techniques in a new context. And since mistakes can be discouraging and possibly even expensive, try doing a "dry run" first for any part of the process you think you might not understand. You'll be glad you did.

Using a Color Copier and Photo-Transfer Paper

Of all the possible methods, I prefer transferring my photos to fabric by using photo-transfer paper and a laser color copier. I find that this is the way I get the greatest clarity and best color. In fact, my photo transfers often look as good as or better than my original photographs.

Photo-transfer paper works on most color photocopiers, but transfer papers do differ. Some produce better color, some create a stiffer transfer on fabric, some cannot be ironed, and some cannot be washed with good results. My favorite transfer paper, chosen after comparing ten different ones, is Photo Transfer Paper from Martingale & Company/That Patchwork Place. It produces great color, adds only slight stiffness to fabric compared to other transfer papers, and you can even iron directly on the images when using steam and high heat. It's also permanent.

We'll cover laser color copiers in greater detail on pages 10–17, but first you'll want to read the following sections to learn about your other options.

Using Transfer Paper Made for Inkjet Printers

Transfer papers for inkjet printers are also available, and many of these papers are now permanent. This has not always been the case. Try a sheet and wash the transfer on fabric just in case. You never know when you might need to wash even a wall hanging if someone splatters something on it. Inkjet printers work differently than laser color copiers. The image they produce on fabric is usually thicker. The reason is the ink itself. Laser color copiers use toner, while inkjet printers use water-soluble inks. In order to make the inks permanent, a coating is placed on top to seal them. This creates a heavier, stiffer image on cloth. But, as with transfer papers for laser color copiers, inkjet papers vary. With an unfamiliar paper, do a test before copying all your photos onto paper you haven't used before.

One advantage of using inkjet transfer paper to create photo transfers on your computer is that, if you have the right software, you can manipulate the photographic images in color, clarity, and effect. These programs let you enlarge, reduce, overlap, and rotate images, and change image coloration in as many ways as you like. In fact, you can experiment to your heart's content. There are many possibilities, and they will only increase as new computer programs become available.

Using Fabric Sheets

Another way of transferring photos to fabric is to transfer the image directly to fabric without the intermediate step of using transfer paper. Fabric sheets, as they are called, are available for this process. They are 8½" x 11" pieces of fabric, white or muslin-colored, and have a paper backing, similar to freezer paper, fused to them. Fabric sheets are fed directly into inkjet-type printers (which would include many home-office "copiers"). The ink is applied directly to the fabric. With some fabric sheets, the images are immediately permanent; with others, you need to treat the image in some way to make the image permanent. Follow the directions provided by the manufacturer. Although the images on the fabric sheets are usually not as clear as those done on transfer paper, they are softer because the ink is applied directly to the fabric.

Which Transfer Medium Should I Use?
Photo-transfer papers and fabric sheets each have advantages and disadvantages. Here's a sample of the pros and cons. You'll want to choose the features that are most important for individual projects.

PHOTO-TRANSFER PAPER FOR LASER COLOR COPIERS
Pro: Highest-quality color and clearest image
Con: Usually needs to be copied in a copy shop which means extra time and money

PHOTO-TRANSFER PAPER FOR INKJET PRINTERS
Pro: No cost for copying if you can use your printer at home
Con: Thickest, stiffest transfer; color quality and permanency vary

FABRIC SHEETS
Pro: Most flexible transfer of image, since ink is applied directly to fabric
Con: Image is not as clear as when using transfer papers; only two options currently available for fabric: white cotton and muslin

Using a Laser Color Copier to Make Photo Transfers

*F*ollow the guidelines for making photo transfers below, but be sure also to read the instructions that come with your particular transfer paper.

Practicing with Your Paper

If you are using a photo-transfer paper for the first time, or one with which you are unfamiliar, try a sheet before committing to the whole pack. Yes, you are technically "wasting" a sheet, but if you discover how good or how difficult the paper is to work with, you could save yourself considerable time and money. Consider the first sheet an investment in your project!

Reducing and Enlarging Photos

If you want to reduce or enlarge your photographs, you can do so in two ways. One is to work with the original photograph and make a photographic reduction or enlargement. The other is to use a copy machine to manipulate the photograph (the less expensive option). In this book I give instructions for the copy-machine method.

It's always a good idea to check the color and size of the photographs after reducing or enlarging them by copying them onto a sheet of regular paper before using the photo-transfer paper. It's much less expensive to pay for a color copy on a regular sheet of paper than to waste a sheet of transfer paper.

Choosing a Photocopy Machine (and Copy Shop)

Laser photocopiers are widely available in most copy centers and also in shops that provide mailing services (those are the ones I use). Always use a laser *color* copier when using photo transfer paper. Don't use a black-and-white copier, even if your photos are black and white. Black-and-white copiers get too hot for photo-transfer paper.

Keep in mind that photo-transfer paper is still a relatively new product. When you make a photo-transfer quilt, you're on the cutting edge, so to speak. Not all shop owners and copy technicians are familiar with transfer paper. And their copy machines are expensive, so they are sometimes reluctant to use something new. You may need to check more than one shop before you find one that will let you try the transfer paper in their machines (and they almost always insist on doing it for you). When you do find a shop, offer to spread the word as a "thank you" to them. In a few years, you'll probably be able to go into any copy shop and they'll not only accept transfer paper but also ask you what kind you prefer. But we're not there yet!

Before You Go to the Copy Shop
If you'd like to figure out how many sheets of photo-transfer paper you'll need before you take your project to the copy shop, consider taping or gluing your photos to 8½" x 11" sheets of regular white paper.

Using the Color Laser Copier

In most copy shops, because the machines are so expensive and the technology is so new, you'll find that you can't make transfers yourself, but will have to have a shop employee make them for you. For this reason, make sure to read the instructions that come with your photo-transfer sheets, and encourage the copy technician to do the same. If he or she doesn't, speak up (nicely). Remind them to mirror-image, and other important guidelines, before they make mistakes.

TIP

Because of the expense and frustration involved in ruining photo-transfer paper, be sure to ask the technician, until you're familiar with each other's work, to do a sample sheet before he or she starts on your actual transfers. You might even want to do one yourself first as a color copy, then have the operator do one on the photo-transfer paper. You can adjust the color settings, etc., at this point. Once you both get the hang of it, it's easier to hand over a whole stack of your precious work and trust that it'll come back to you just as you'd desire. For this reason, it makes sense to patronize copy establishments that regularly serve quilters.

Whether you're using the color laser copier yourself or entrusting the job to a copy technician, you'll want to be familiar with the process. To make a photo transfer, place photos facedown on the glass. If you don't plan to enlarge them, feel free to butt photos up against one another to maximize use of the transfer paper.

Feed each sheet of transfer paper, one at a time, into the copier using the bypass tray. Copy onto the shiny side of the transfer paper (if your paper is watermarked, it's the side without the design). Avoid using paper that has been bent or creased—this will affect the quality of your transfer and may also jam the machine.

Choose your image-quality selections carefully (see "Key Settings for the Color Laser Copier" on page 12) and make sure that the copy machine is set on "mirror image," so that your image will transfer correctly. (It makes two transitions: original to reverse image and reverse image to final image, so be careful that lettering and familiar faces both "read" correctly in the result.)

TIP

Paper photo transfers are delicate and should be handled with care. The color sits lightly on the surface of the transfer paper and is easily damaged. Once the image has been transferred to fabric it will be more durable, but while on paper it's fragile and vulnerable to inadvertent scratches or gouges from keys, fingernails, pens, and other objects. For this reason, I prefer cutting around my images with sharp scissors rather than using rotary-cutting equipment. I get precision without the risk of nicking transfers with an acrylic ruler.

Key Settings for the Color Laser Copier

The primary reason you're making a photo-transfer quilt is to show off particular photos, because you love them or the subjects they depict. However, some attention should be paid to the quality of the photos you're using. Because most of us are not professional photographers, most (or all) of the photographs we have are snapshot quality. They may be darker or lighter than we'd like, less clear, or cluttered with unwanted background objects. By trying one or more of the options that follow, we may be able to improve our results. Sometimes you can even improve on your original!

Keep in mind that laser color copiers vary. Different color laser copiers offer similar features, but they don't all call them by the same names or achieve them with the same buttons. So use the following tips as guidelines only.

Output Color

Use "full color" rather than the automatic "auto color." If you're copying in black and white, press "black." You can also use "single color," in which you select a color you want and the photo is reproduced in various shades of that color.

Pink, blue, green, and yellow single-color copies

To get the image on a same-colored background, try adding a black piece of paper behind the item being photocopied (see samples below).

Pink, blue, green, and yellow single-color copies made with black backgrounds

Original leaf

Three-Color

Three-color means the machine uses equal amounts of the three colors used in full-color printing—cyan (blue), magenta (red), and yellow—to make black. This process creates a black that is softer and more natural than the black we usually see. Selecting this option doesn't affect the other colors in the picture, but because the black is softer the overall effect is that the picture is now softer in tone and lower in contrast.

Old-fashioned

The old-fashioned function changes a color or black-and-white image to sepia tones, like the dark brown pigments of an antique photo. Try a sample first—sometimes the tones don't reproduce in brown but in blue or another color. Another way to get sepia tones is to select "brown" in the "Single Color" setting (above).

Lighter/Darker

Because images naturally darken a little when transferred to fabric, you may want to compensate for this by adjusting the setting of your original photo transfer by 1 to 3 levels, to produce a lighter transfer. Depending on your photo, the change may not be too noticeable, but it's particularly important with photographs of people, where flesh tones or the color of a blouse might be important to retain. If the background of your photograph is dark, pay particular attention to lightening the setting of the photo transfer. (You might want to do a test run here to understand this principle better.)

Document Type

Select the "Photograph" rather than the "Text" button.

Edit/Mirror Image

Select this so photos read correctly on fabric. This is an important step, which—if overlooked—can result in photos reading "backward" on the finished quilt.

Copy Quality

Two key settings are "Color Saturation" and "Sharpness." "Color Saturation" affects the intensity of the colors and can improve the colors in your original photograph. "Sharpness" adds clarity to any photograph, out of focus or not. It can also make a slightly out-of-focus picture clearer. I often use the highest settings available for both saturation and sharpness. Be sure to do a sample first to check the "trueness" of your colors.

Reduce/Enlarge

A larger photograph will show up better than a smaller one, to a certain extent. A small 3" x 5" photo might not transition well to 8" x 10", so enlarge within reason.

The "Reduce" and "Enlarge" settings change the size of your photo. You can select an exact percentage (reduce to 75 percent, for example), or many machines can automatically adjust for the output size you want (such as 5" x 7"). Do a sample to check the size before using transfer paper.

TIP

Check your work. Because every time you manipulate a photo you're introducing changes, it's important—if you want to be precise—to check the quality of your work as you go. If you change color, clarity, etc., try running a sample copy, even if it's on copy paper rather than transfer paper, to see the overall effect before proceeding. It may save time, money, and aggravation, and keep you loving, not dreading, the creative process.

Troubleshooting Transfers

* **Does the transfer have horizontal streaks running across it, or bands of uneven color?** This not a problem with the transfer paper. The drum of the color copier needs to be serviced.

* **Is the image too light?** Adjust the "Lighten/ Darken" button.

* **Color not good?** Make sure you've pressed "Full Color," not "Auto Color." Possibly adjust "Color Saturation."

* **Color flakes off the transfer paper?** The ink has not been applied properly to the transfer paper. This is most likely a copy machine problem. Try another copy machine. (Be sure to protect your delicate photo transfer after it's made, though, from accidental scraping and gouging.)

* **Is the image too fuzzy?** If your original is sharper, try adjusting the copier's "Sharpness" button. If you're enlarging greatly from a clear original, be aware that images distort over the size of the enlargement, and consider making a slightly smaller enlargement for greater clarity.

* **Do any of the words read backwards? (Or is a face in profile looking the other way?)** This is how it should be. They should read backwards at this point so they will ultimately read correctly on the fabric.

Selecting Fabric for Transfers

Now that you've made your transfers, it's time to decide what kind of fabric you'll transfer them to. Tightly woven, white or light-colored 100 percent cotton is the usual and reliable choice. Whatever fabric you choose, keep in mind that those with a tight weave, such as Pima cotton, work best. For a discussion of other fabric options, see "Transferring to Special Fabrics" on page 16.

Don't prewash your fabric. The threads are straighter and the fabric will be smoother right off the bolt. Even though you're not prewashing your fabric, the photo-transfer process will stabilize it so that it won't shrink when washed.

Cutting Fabric for Your Transfers

If you have more than one picture on a sheet of transfer paper, cut them apart. Then cut pieces of fabric at least 1" larger on each side than the photo to be transferred. For example, cut a 4" x 6" rectangle of fabric for a 3" x 5" photograph. Why do I add 1" extra when I really need only ½" (assuming a ¼" seam allowance)? Because it's difficult to center the transfer on the fabric during pressing. Also, as the pressing surface you're working on heats up with repeated transfers, the transfer paper tends to curl, making it even more difficult to center. So, allow for extra fabric. But I seldom measure each one of my photo transfers. Instead, I place my transfers, one by one, on fabric, and generously cut around them freehand with my rotary cutter. Although this might waste some fabric, I find it's the fastest method.

Using Heat to Transfer Your Images onto Fabric

Household Iron or Heat Press?

To transfer your image to fabric, you can use either a reliable iron you know and trust, or a heat press (such as those found in T-shirt shops and at some quilt and copy shops). If you use a heat press, set it at 375°; if you use an iron, set it at the highest temperature (but with no steam). Be fairly meticulous about removing any lint from the fabric you're using, so a lump or nub doesn't show through later in your image. (This is especially important with images of people's faces.) If desired, you can press the fabric for a few seconds to eliminate wrinkles, but if you're using a heat press, in particular, this isn't always necessary. The heat press will remove any wrinkles during the transfer process.

Using a Heat Press

Place your photo-transfer images facedown on the fabric. When using a heat press, you can press two or three images at one time. Press images for twenty-five seconds. Peel paper off immediately.

TIP

If transfers must be placed exactly on a piece of fabric, sometimes I take an extra step of pressing them lightly with an iron before transferring them to fabric using the press. (This is particularly important with lettering or fine lines that you want to preserve, such as line drawings or fragile illustrations, and sometimes when placing images on-point.) I pressed first with an iron in *Cookie Jar* (page 73) to keep the letters from shifting before I transferred them with the heat press.

Using an Iron

If you're using an iron, press one image at a time, placing your photo-transfer image facedown on the fabric. Press on a firm, smooth, flat surface, such as a tabletop or a piece of shelving such as melamine. Don't use your padded ironing board. See following section, "Ironing Pitfalls." To achieve maximum pressure, you may want to lower your pressing surface so you can place as much of your weight over the iron as possible. Depending on your fabric, you may also need to adjust the pressing time. Position smaller images directly under the sole plate. With sufficient pressure, even the holes in the iron shouldn't be a problem. For large images, move the iron to press the entire image, holding it down in each position for the required amount of time and slightly overlapping your previous pressing area. Reheat the entire sheet of paper before peeling it off.

IRONING PITFALLS

Yes, you can use a household iron to transfer photographs to fabric. But there are five factors that directly affect the quality of the transfer.

Heat: The highest heat is desired, but the exact temperature an iron reaches is unknown, and varies somewhat from iron to iron. Older irons often get hotter than newer irons. You have no control over this variable.

Pressure: You'll want to use as much pressure as possible, each and every time you do a transfer. Once you've gotten the hang of it, you still need to keep the pressure up and not relax.

Surface: You must use a surface that's firm, smooth, and flat. All three words are equally important. You need something firm and flat to force the transfer inks onto fabric. Cushy ironing boards don't work. Neither does plywood, which is firm and flat, but not smooth. You'll get wood-grain swirls or lines in your transfer. Using any varnished surface risks melting the finish off onto your fabric. Try using a cookie sheet, if your cookie sheets are still flat and not curved from years of use. Cookie sheets are firm and smooth, and because the metal heats up it helps the transfer process.

Pressing Time: Lightweight fabrics require less pressing time than heavier ones. The composition of the fabric (100 percent cotton vs. cotton blends or satin) also affects the pressing time. Pressing a lightweight fabric for twenty-five seconds may scorch it. Pima cotton, which is a good choice for photo transfers, is lighter in weight than cotton sateen, for example, and may need to be pressed for only fifteen or twenty seconds.

Fabric Texture: Some fabrics have smooth, satiny finishes, others have a more linen-like, bumpy texture. Your iron will read bumpy fabrics as a topographic map—a landscape of peaks and valleys—and without sufficient pressure, might miss transferring the color to the valleys.

TIP

If you're planning to do your photo transfers with an iron instead of a heat press, be prepared to make some samples first. I like to cut up a single "sample" photo transfer into two, three, or four pieces, and practice pressing each piece until I have determined the correct amount of time needed to get a good transfer—taking into consideration my iron, the pressing surface I'm using, and the fabric I've chosen. If the fabric causes problems, I consider changing to a smoother fabric, if necessary. Practicing also helps me check to be sure I'm using sufficient pressure.

Peeling Off the Paper Backing

It's important to peel the backing off the photo transfer paper immediately after pressing, while the paper is still hot. If the paper cools down too much and becomes hard to peel, simply reheat for a few seconds before trying again. Once the paper backing is removed, you can smooth out any distortions in the fabric by reheating slightly. Some fabrics, like satins, distort more than cottons; you can easily press them back into shape with an iron.

Do Transferred Images Need Special Care?

Once images have been transferred to suitable fabric, it's remarkable how durable they can be. The color doesn't peel off, so long as the transfer was good, and you can both wash and iron them to remove wrinkles. (Wrinkles on a photo transfer usually show up as white creases across the face of the transfer—momentarily disturbing, but nothing permanent. They iron out nicely.)

You may not want or need to wash a photo transfer—but it's nice to know you can, especially if something gets accidentally spilled on your quilt or wall hanging. To wash transfer fabric, first consult the directions for the specific transfer paper you're using. In general, you want to treat transfer fabric as you would any other fine textile. Try spot-washing it (by daubing), or wash by hand with a mild soap. Use cool or warm water, but don't use any bleach or fabric softener. Lay your transfer or quilt flat to dry.

Transferring to Special Fabrics

Silk

When I made *Three Generations* (page 92), I used silk peau de soie (a matte-finished satin that has some body to it). The fine weave of the satin made the photos so clear and sharp that they look like original photographs. Before transferring the images with a heat press, I used an iron to press the fabric to keep it flat, and then lightly pressed the images in place so they would not shift. Then I switched to the heat press, and lowered the pressing time from 25 seconds to 20, but kept the temperature the same (375°).

Linen

When I made *Meow!* (page 58), I used a yellow-and-white linen in a checked pattern. The weave added a vintage look to the old-fashioned images. Because linen fabrics have an open weave and are somewhat stretchy, I prewashed and dried it before applying the transfer. I like to cut photo transfers close to their edges, as I did below with *Meow!*'s cats. I discovered that the weave and texture of the linen makes the edges of the photo transfer almost disappear. The result was the look of an expensive, preprinted panel. I pressed this transfer for 25 seconds at 375° using a heat press.

Trim each photo transfer
close to the image's edge.

Wool

To get the best-quality transfer onto a textured fabric like wool, use a heat press rather than an iron. In this case, I prewashed the wool in the washing machine (hottest temperature, most agitation), then dried it in the dryer on the hottest setting to "felt" it. By first boiling or felting the wool in this way, you ensure that exposed seam allowances won't fray. To transfer the woodcuts, I pressed the transfers for 25 seconds at 375° using a heat press.

Osnaburg

Cookie Jar (page 73) was made with Osnaburg. It is a muslin-colored cotton fabric with an open weave and occasional flecks of darker nubs, and gives a wonderful texture to landscape and seascape photographs, because it looks a bit like artist's canvas. It also works well for photographs and images other than people. I don't use it for photographs of people because a noticeable, nubby weave is not attractive in people's faces. Consider prewashing the fabric if you expect there's a chance you'll have to wash the quilt. As with wool, use a heat press if at all possible to get the best-quality transfer on this bumpy fabric. I pressed for 20 seconds at 375° using a heat press.

Repairing an Antique Quilt

You can use photo transfers in a unique way: to repair an antique quilt. There may be times when you want to repair a portion of an older quilt, but are unable to match the fabric in need of repair. In that case, by copying a portion of fabric from the quilt onto photo-transfer paper and then to fabric you can create a small piece similar in color (or faded color) to your original. Put the quilt on the glass of the color copier, and don't forget to mirror-image the design so it will read correctly. Transfer as usual. Now, stitch your new "fabric" onto the quilt over the damaged area (like an appliqué). The transferred copy will be a little stiffer than the original fabric, but otherwise may do the trick.

Remember that fabric designs are protected by copyright. I'd recommend not copying anything current or recently available for purchase, because that could be a violation of copyright law.

Getting Started

You've chosen images and transferred them to fabric. Now it's time to choose coordinating fabrics and design your quilt.

Photo quilts are special because of the photographs. With all the photo-transfer quilts I've made, I've never had anyone comment on my fabric choices, or choices for blocks. What they comment on is the photographs, because that's what their eye is drawn to, and that's the part of the quilt that is personal and therefore meaningful to them. You and I may worry about fabric colors, which blocks to choose, whether photos should be the centers of blocks, whether or not to appliqué the photos, etc. But the people who will see your finished quilt will notice the photographs, not the blocks, the fabrics, or the settings.

Of course, your photo-transfer quilt will be unique. No one can make a quilt with your treasured photographs like you can. And, since special photos are an important part of this quilt, it has the potential to become an heirloom that will be passed down for generations. Just thinking about these things is enough to make a quilter stop before she starts! But don't stop—do get started.

One thing to keep in mind as you design your memory quilt is that there's no such thing as a perfect quilt. I can honestly say that I've never made one. There's never been a quilt I've made where I didn't later wish that I'd changed something about it. So let go of the idea of perfection. Perfectionism will not only keep you from getting started on your quilt, it will also block your creativity when your quilt is under way. It's obviously much easier to create when you're relaxed. Your ideas will flow much better. I think it's better to create an *imperfect* (but well-loved!) photo-transfer quilt than to wait for years for the perfect idea, which may never

come. Rather than leaving your photos to gather dust in a box, where no one can enjoy them, you'll be creating a thing of beauty that will bring joy to the people you share it with. How much better just to get started!

Finding Inspiration

Study your photo transfers to find inspiration and ideas. What do they suggest? Let's say you notice you're collecting a group of photos of your spouse fishing. What about appliquéing or piecing a fish to go along with the photos on the quilt? This is the time to be creative. Play with ideas. Brainstorm! There's no one way to make a wonderful quilt. Instead, there are many ways. And you get to choose the one you like best!

Don't rush this part of the process, but allow it to take some time, and gel. You need time to let your ideas form naturally, and to consider which ideas might work or might not, for various reasons. Allow yourself time enough to contemplate all the possibilities, in a way that you can't once the process is further under way. That said, don't wait forever. At some point, you have to take the first step and just begin. Trust that you'll sort things out as your work progresses.

General Guidelines

❧ Consider your skill level and personal preferences. Do you feel more comfortable piecing or appliquéing? If you've chosen to piece, do you like the look of simple frames around your photographs, or do you want to make blocks to surround or frame your photo transfers? Do you want the photos to be at the centers of blocks or to alternate with blocks?

- Remember, your photographs should be the stars of your quilt. They're the reason you're making the quilt, so they should be what you see first. Make your photographs the lightest, brightest, or darkest things in your quilt.

- Emphasize your images. Pare away excess background around your image to accentuate the focal point. But don't cut up your original photograph to do this. Trim the photo transfer instead.

Trim photo transfers close
to the edge of the focal point.

- Since the photographs are the central focus in these quilts, elaborate, complex piecing isn't necessary. That isn't to say that the blocks you make can't be complex (if you'd like them to be), just that it isn't necessary. Perhaps by now you'll recognize that I keep emphasizing that the photographs are the most important element in these quilts. Everything else, piecing included, is secondary. The fabrics, even the style of blocks, are there to support and help show off the photographs.

Designing Your Quilt

Quiltmakers use different design techniques. Some choose and play with fabric, getting ideas as they work, others like to sketch their ideas on paper. If you go the sketching route, don't restrict yourself by considering your sketch a "recipe" to be followed precisely. Allow yourself the freedom to change your mind while you're working on the quilt, experimenting with the other ideas that occur to you as time goes on. Quilters are very visual. Sometimes we plan something out that we think should look good, but later—when we actually see it—we no longer think it does. That means it's time to let go of the original idea. Why hang onto something that's no longer working?

One product you might find useful in designing your blocks is called Grid Grip. It's a combination of freezer paper and graph paper. You can draw your block design on the paper and then cut the different design elements of the block apart. Next, you lightly press the pieces onto fabric (if you press on the wrong side of the fabric, you're reversing your image; if you press on the right side of the fabric, you aren't), add a seam allowance, and stitch the pieces together. Last, peel off the Grid Grip. It works especially well to stabilize bias edges. With this product, if you can draw the block on paper, you can make it. You can also reuse it numerous times. See "Resources" on page 95.

Choosing Coordinating Fabrics

If possible, choose your quiltmaking fabrics *after* your photo transfers are made. Why? Because sometimes colors change somewhat in the process of transferring onto fabric. A blouse in a photograph may show as a cool bluish red, but by the time the photo's transferred onto fabric it may appear as a warm orange-red instead. If you've committed to a range of fabrics ahead of time, based on the colors in the original photographs, or even based on what you see on transfer paper before being transferred to fabric, you may find that the colors you've chosen are no longer a perfect match. This doesn't always happen, but it happens often enough that I prefer to wait until my photos are on fabric before I choose the fabrics to coordinate with them.

Fabric Styles

There's a variety of fabric *styles* to choose from, and you can choose any you prefer: solids, florals, plaids, batiks, '30s prints, even novelty prints (if they aren't too busy). With both color and pattern, it helps to evaluate the color and complexity of your original photographs, and use these as a guideline when selecting the fabrics you'll use.

Coordinate fabric colors with your photo transfers.

Working with Color

Use the colors you see in your photographs as a guide for the colors you choose for fabrics. When you do this, you not only complement the colors in the photograph, you also help the colors pop out and therefore you see the photographs better, and that's the point.

You can also use a color wheel to see what a color's complement is (the color directly opposite it on the wheel). Adding a complementary color also can help make its complement stand out.

With photographs in neutral colors, such as black-and-white or sepia, you have more options. You can choose any fabric colors you like, keeping the above guidelines in mind. It's also possible to beautifully combine color, black-and-white, and sepia photographs in the same quilt. For an example, see *Gone Fishing* on page 43.

When choosing fabrics to go with your photos, choose what you see, not what you know. Pin your photos on fabric on the wall or prop them up against the back of a couch or chair, and step away. What colors do you see? Be objective and choose the colors you really see, not the ones you know are there. For example, your mom's dress in the photo may be a beautiful shade of blue, with yellow flowers on it. But from a distance, can you really see the yellow flowers, or does it appear as a field entirely of blue? If the yellow disappears, from a distance, don't choose yellow fabric. Why? Because the yellow fabric will stand out, and won't look like it's coordinating with anything. Instead of enhancing and helping to show off the photographs, it will compete with them for attention.

It's possible to use bright fabrics in your photo-transfer quilts, but restrict them to accent colors. For example, you might try creating a hint of color in the background that pulls (and highlights) a color from the photo transfer itself. In *A Garden of Memories* (page 38), notice that bright colors work well as a thin border around a photograph. To ensure that bright colors aren't too bright or overwhelming, evaluate them from a distance—for example, pinned to a design wall—before cutting and sewing.

Previewing Fabrics

As you preview your photographs and fabrics, step back. Look at them from a distance, the way you'll see the finished quilt on the wall. Things change at a distance. Remember, your photographs should be the stars.

Despite careful efforts, sometimes your colors just won't work. I looked at photos of our goat Peanut and our rabbit Eddie, already transferred to fabric, to choose fabric colors. I chose dark gray and blue, similar to the colors I saw in Peanut's coat; gold similar to Eddie's coat; and red, the complement of the green grass (see below).

Photo transfer of Peanut and Eddie

The coordinating fabrics I chose: red to complement the green grass, and blue, gold, and dark gray to match the photo transfer.

I found that the gold, although it helped make the rabbit noticeable, also drew my eyes away from the photo.

The gold border overwhelms the photo transfer.

I also discovered that the green grass was brighter than the animals. I struggled to calm it down, and found that red, surprisingly, did so because it was similarly bright and was also a complement to green.

Adding red corner squares makes the green less noticeable.

Notice how the colors in the finished quilt, *Best Friends: Peanut the Pygmy Goat and Eddie Rabbit* (page 69) differ from my original colors.

Framing Your Images

The fabrics you choose to position next to your photo transfers should be in a different value than the backgrounds of the photos. You want the viewer's eyes to find the photo, not the fabric; so be sure to frame the photos in contrasting values, much as you would frame a photo with a matte. You'll want to make it clear where the photo ends and the fabric frame begins. Look at the following photos and fabrics to see examples of good contrast.

Your fabrics need to complement the photographs, not conflict with them. Brightly contrasting, busy, large-scale fabrics compete with the photos, and viewers don't know which to look at first. Remember that it's the special photographs you want the viewer to see: the fabrics need to support the photographs, not the other way around.

Light background with medium frame

Dark background with light frame

Medium background with light frame

Light background with dark frame

Dark background with medium frame

Medium background with dark frame

Dark background (top) and light background (bottom) with medium frame

Busy, large-scale floral borders steal attention from the photo transfer.

Framing Your Photos

Your photos may all be just the size you need, but more often they won't. It's much more common for people's special photographs to be a collection of different sizes. There are a number of ways to work with photos of different dimensions.

* Decide not to alter the sizes of the photos. You can easily appliqué transfers of different sizes to a single background, or you can piece them into blocks and add fabric to fill the spaces between blocks. See *Fabric and Fotos* by Janice Eggleston on pages 46–47.

* Resize all your photos to the same size, by enlarging or reducing them, when you copy them onto transfer paper. This is your most costly and time-consuming option.

* Once your photos are all on transfer paper or fabric, you could trim them down to the same size. But remember that this is a little bit of living dangerously—the trimmed photos might not look equally good, and you might risk trimming off something important to the visual balance or composition.

* Add fabric to the quilt blocks, more on some and less on others, to make everything a uniform size. This is the method I use most often.

Once you've decided on the size of your photos, the next step is to frame them. You want your frames to enhance the photos and help them stand out. Here are just a few examples of framing options.

Single frame

Double frame

Checkerboard frame

Photo-album frame

Triangle frame,
horizontal photo

Triangle frame,
vertical photo

Photos as the Centers of Pieced Blocks

Have you ever noticed that the centers of most pieced blocks are square? But most photographs are rectangular, with two sides larger than the others. (The most popular sizes are 3" x 5", 4" x 6", 5" x 7", and 8" x 10".) You can sometimes trim a photograph to a square without eliminating anything crucial, but it's not always possible. Sometimes cropping really changes how the photograph looks, and not in a way that improves it. The good news is that many blocks traditionally made with square centers can be changed to accommodate rectangular ones without spoiling their look.

Off-center Log Cabin

Attic Windows

Courthouse Steps

Checkerboard or One Patch

Courthouse Steps variation—
double frame

Four Patch

If your photos are rectangular, and the blocks you choose don't adapt easily to rectangles, you'll need to square up your photos. To do this, consider the settings shown below.

Add fabric to the photo
to make the center square.

Trim the photo
to make the center square.

Photos That Alternate with Pieced Blocks

The same principle applies if you're alternating your rectangular photos with either square or rectangular blocks. You'll need to make your photos the same size (both height and width) as your pieced blocks. You can do this either by trimming the photos or by adding strips of fabric to the blocks.

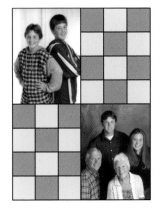

Trim photos to fit blocks.

Add strips to photos to fit blocks.

Fitting Together Photos of Different Sizes

If your photos, blocks, or the resulting combinations of your photos and blocks are all different sizes, you'll need to consider how to fit them together. Follow this guideline: if it's too big, trim it; if it's too small, add fabric.

1. Arrange your finished blocks on a flat surface, preferably a Quilt Wall (similar to thick fleece) hung vertically rather than laid horizontally on the floor (see "Resources" on page 95). Your eye is better able to make design choices on a vertical surface, without the challenge of perspective or foreshortening. Move your blocks around until you get a pleasing arrangement. At this point, pay no attention to the blocks' individual sizes.

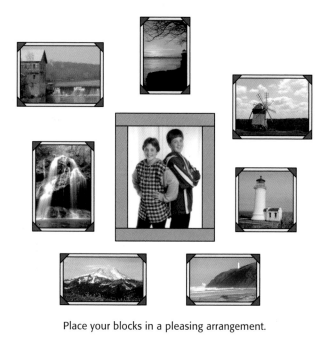

Place your blocks in a pleasing arrangement.

2. Now, start with any corner where two blocks are next to each other. If they're not the same size (and they probably won't be), you'll need to make the smaller one as tall as the larger one. To do this, sew some extra strips or squares to the top or bottom of the smaller block until it's a little taller than it needs to be. Then trim the excess.

Working with adjacent blocks, add fabric elements as needed to make them an equal height.

3. If you don't like the look of two or more photo-transfer blocks next to each other, sew fabric spacers in between, and then trim the excess. These spacers can take the form of extra strips, squares, or pieced blocks.

4. Add extra strips if desired.

5. Work in sections of twos or threes, then put these sections together in rows using the principle mentioned above: if there's too little, add; if something's too big, trim.

Add next block.

Add strips or squares to shorter unit.

Cut off excess.

Sew sections together to make a row.

6. Fit the rows together, adding segments or trimming edges as needed. If you need to add filler pieces, consider using a block that complements your theme. For example, a sailboat block may be used to fill space in a quilt commemorating a summer vacation.

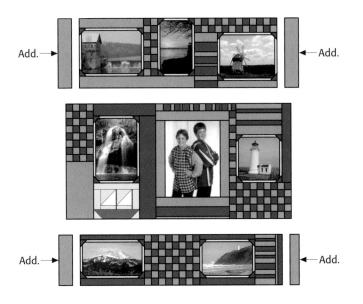
Add. →   ← Add.

Add. →   ← Add.

7. Sew the rows together to complete the quilt top.

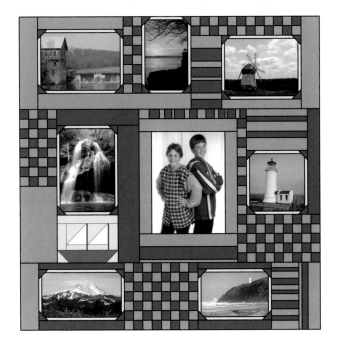

Appliquéing Photo Transfers

You can also appliqué your photos onto, rather than piece them into, a quilt. Appliqué actually offers you more placement flexibility than piecing does. You can often fit more photos onto your quilt when you appliqué them. Try placing them askew or overlapping them for added interest.

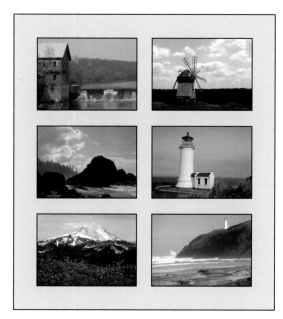

Straight Setting

Askew Setting

Overlapping, Askew Setting

Finishing Your Quilt

This section is your opportunity to review the basics, and to learn a few techniques special to photo-transfer quilts.

Borders

For plain borders (without corner squares), first measure the quilt top vertically through the center. Cut two border strips to match the measurement, then sew them to the sides of the quilt top. Measure the quilt top again horizontally through the center, including the borders just added. Cut two border strips to match the measurement, then sew them to the top and bottom edges. Press the seam allowances toward the borders.

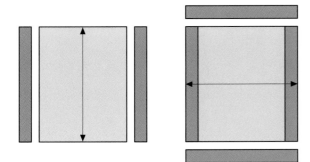

For borders with corner squares, measure the quilt top through the center, both horizontally and vertically. Add border strips to the sides edges first. Sew corner squares to the remaining borders and add these to the top and bottom edges of the quilt. Press seam allowances toward the borders.

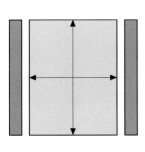 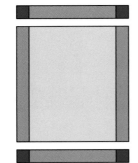

If you need to piece border strips to make them fit your quilt top, join them with a diagonal seam. Trim the seam allowances to ¼" and press the seams open.

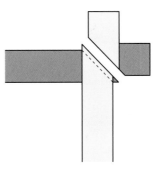

Backing

Cut backing at least 4" larger than your quilt top.

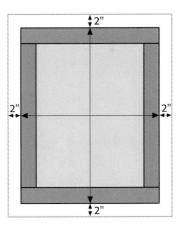

If this measurement is wider than the width of your backing fabric, piece two lengths or two widths of backing fabric together.

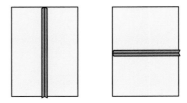

If the backing needs to be only a few inches wider than the quilt top, I often add a strip down the middle. The strip can be a single piece of fabric or it can be pieced from leftovers.

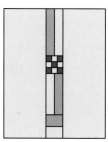

Layering and Basting

The quilt sandwich is made of the quilt top, batting, and backing.

1. Unroll the batting and let it relax overnight before you layer your quilt. Cut the batting 4" larger than the quilt top.

2. Place the backing, wrong side up, on a large table. Use masking tape to anchor the backing to the table. Make sure the backing is flat and wrinkle-free, but be careful not to stretch it out of shape.

3. Place the batting on top of the backing, smoothing out all the wrinkles.

4. Center the pressed quilt top, right side up, on top of the batting. Smooth out any wrinkles. Make sure the quilt-top edges are parallel to the backing edges.

5. Baste with needle and thread if hand quilting, or with safety pins if machine quilting. To quilt, start in the center and work toward the outside edges.

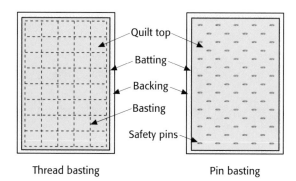

Thread basting   Pin basting

Quilting a Photo-Transfer Quilt

Photo transfers created with transfer paper (not transfers made directly onto fabric) add some stiffness to fabric. How much stiffness depends on the transfer paper you're using. Transfers that add little stiffness to fabric can be quilted through easily, even by hand, although you won't be able to load your needle with stitches. Consider the following suggestions:

❧ Quilt by hand or machine inside the transfers. Stitch along figures' outlines or around backgrounds behind people or objects to make them stand out in relief.

The quilting around this leaf emphasizes it.

❧ Quilt ¼" from the edges of the transfers. The stitching line will create an additional frame.

❧ Consider matching quilting designs with the subject of the quilt. Becky Kraus quilted paws in the corners of the *My Baby Neville* quilt on page 61.

Quilted paws complement this quilt's focus on Neville the dog.

The larger the photo transfer, the more it will have a tendency to "pooch out" after the material around it has been quilted. Be careful not to stretch the fabrics (you can't stretch the transfer) as you quilt. Stretching can make things worse. If you find this to be a problem, try quilting inside the transfer itself.

Binding

My preferred binding is a double-layer, straight-grain binding that finishes to ¼". Don't trim excess batting and backing before adding the binding. I use a double-fold bias binding only when I want to change the direction of the binding print.

1. For straight-grain strips, cut enough 2"-wide strips across the width of the fabric to go around the perimeter of the quilt. For bias strips, cut 2"-wide strips at a 45-degree angle to the straight grain. Sew the strips end to end with a diagonal seam.

2. Cut one end at a 45-degree angle. You don't need to measure this, just eyeball it. Fold about ¼" of the angled end to the wrong side, then press. Press the entire strip in half lengthwise, with wrong sides together.

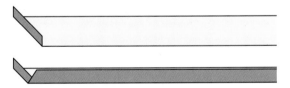

3. Start on a straight edge, not in a corner. Place the angled end of the binding along the quilt top, aligning the raw edges of the binding with the raw edges of the quilt top. Using a ¼"-wide seam allowance, begin machine stitching about 3" from the angled end. Backstitch to secure.

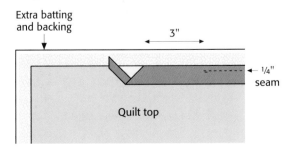

4. When you get close to the corner, insert a pin ¼" from the edge (eyeball it), sew up to the pin, and backstitch.

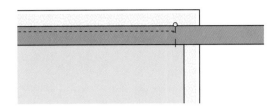

5. Remove the quilt from the machine. Fold the binding up, away from the quilt, then back down so the fold aligns with the edge you just stitched. Align the raw edges of the binding with the next raw edge of the quilt. Begin stitching at the very edge. Repeat with the remaining corners.

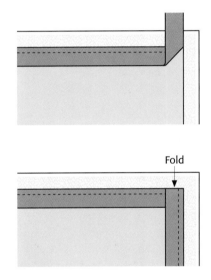

6. When you get close to where you started, insert the binding strip inside the angled end; trim if it's too long. Continue stitching a little past where you began.

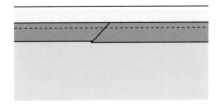

7. Trim the batting and backing even with the edge of the quilt top.

8. Finish the back by hand with a slip stitch, matching the thread color to the binding. In the corners, there will be a natural miter on the front and you will fold a miter on the back.

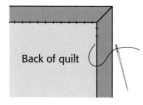

Back of quilt

Embellishing Photo-Transfer Quilts

Before adding embellishments, consider how you plan to use your quilt. Most photo-transfer quilts will end up as wall hangings, and as such can be embellished more than bed or lap quilts. Popular embellishments include buttons, ribbons, lace, and charms. You could also use pins, costume jewelry, patches, emblems, and award ribbons. You might choose your embellishments based on theme, period, or mood.

In *Meow!* (page 58), I added pearl-type buttons and lace to complement the Victorian images.

Using Photographs to Create Labels

If you're reluctant to make a whole photo-transfer quilt, try using just one photo to make a label. Do you have one of your grandmother's antique quilts? How about a picture of her? If you transfer that treasured photo to fabric and then appliqué it to the back of her quilt, your special label will become an integral part of that quilt's history. This is a unique way to blend the traditional with the contemporary. By adding a photo transfer (a relatively new technique) to her quilt (a wonderful example of tradition), you've made an heirloom even more special.

Labels can be any size. I often use a leftover photo from the front of the quilt to create a label for the back. To make a label you'll need an image transferred to fabric, light-colored fabric to write on, and a fine-point permanent marker (size .03 or .05) in black or a dark color. Or you could embroider the lettering with size-8 perle cotton and a chenille needle. Add any embellishments, fabrics, blocks, or parts of blocks you have left over from making the quilt top.

Materials for *Meow!* quilt label

Play with the arrangement of photographs, lettering, strips, blocks, and embellishments. Remember that you don't necessarily have to piece your photo transfer into the label, you could appliqué it on instead.

Although you can write (or stitch) as much as you desire, always include at least your name, city, state, and the year you finished your quilt. Consider the lettering placement. Your lettering can be formatted as a paragraph or written around the edge of an appliquéd shape or photograph.

Try different options. Don't forget that labels can be any size. And if something is too big, cut it off. If it's too little, add on.

Think of your label as a puzzle. There isn't a right or wrong way to put it together. You'll make a more creative label if you allow yourself to play with the possibilities.

50th Anniversary, A Golden Memory by Bonnie Pittrof, 1999, Mukilteo, Washington, 43½" x 43½".

This anniversary quilt was created in honor of my mom and dad. Their wedding photos display an aura of elegance typical of the time, and the five photos show the traditional wedding and include the bridal party at the altar, the cake-cutting, and the first dance. Each photo was framed with assorted trims, including lace, ribbons, and flowers. On the back of the quilt I included an early photo from when my parents were first dating and a roller-skating button to commemorate the way they met. There is also a special pocket containing a bookmark memento from their fiftieth-anniversary party, a special card, and a music box. The label on the pocket has a poem I wrote with a message I am passing down to my children.

Sisters in Alaska by Linda Thomas, 1998, Everett, Washington, 54" x 65".

This quilt was made for my only sister, Sally, to commemorate the cruise we took together to Alaska. The blue fabric in the quilt symbolizes the ocean, the deep blue of the many glaciers, and is Sally's favorite color. The pictures are reminders of the wonderful time we shared, along with our husbands. One picture will even remind her of the fish that didn't get away! Although we live on opposite sides of the country, we can stay close through the memories we share of this wonderful trip.

We Still Miss You, Mom by Nancy "Nan" Naubert, 1999, Tacoma, Washington, 33" x 38".
In memory of Mildred A. Barnhart Naubert, October 24, 1918–January 8, 1959.

I had always wanted to do a quilt as a memorial of my mother. When a photograph of her came out of the blue from a cousin in Texas and coincided with a lecture and workshop on photo-transfer quilts by Sandy Bonsib, I knew it was time. This was a very therapeutic project for me—memories unfolded and stories were retold.

The music fabric represents Mom's love of music, and a photo of her six children shows her legacy. The white stars represent her children: four twirl in one direction (the boys), two in the opposite direction (the girls). A red star represents our father. There are no pictures of Mom in her last years, but I was told that when I was forty I looked very much like her. This quilt now hangs in my office.

Great White Fleet by Bonnie Lippincott Gallagher, 1999, Sandy, Oregon, 46" x 46".

From December 16, 1907, to February 22, 1909, sixteen battleships and 14,000 men of the United States Navy steamed around the world in a grand display of American sea power. They covered 43,000 miles and made twenty ports of call on six continents. The battleships were painted a pristine white with gilded scrollwork on their bows, and later became known as the "Great White Fleet."

The postcards used in this quilt have been in my family for many years. My father was a career naval officer, and the military history of my family dates back to the Revolutionary War. The quilt was a Christmas gift for my mother and is a tribute to my father's naval career.

A Garden of Memories by Linda Cooper, 2000, Friday Harbor, Washington, 53" x 64".

I wanted to incorporate my parents' portraits into a traditional quilt pattern for their fifty-ninth anniversary. My mother is a passionate gardener, so I chose the Garden Twist pattern from In the Beginning, a Seattle quilt shop. I appliquéd same-size portraits into the center hexagons, then inset an inscription in the center diamond. The contrast of the solid cranberry around the photos directs your eye to the family pictures.

Krissy's Quilt by Debbie Aldridge, 1998, Davis, California, 73" x 88".

I made this quilt for my son's girlfriend, Krissy, as a graduation gift. Krissy likes putting together picture collages for herself and her friends, and collaging seemed a good way to make a photo quilt. Krissy gathered pictures from her life for me without knowing what I was going to do with them. I scanned them, sized them on the computer, and printed them out. Since the pictures are on point, I had to extend the photos on the computer to cover the edges. I picked feminine fabrics from Moda's "Folk Art Wedding" collection and used a pattern I found in *Better Homes and Gardens Quilting* magazine. As I am a photographer by profession, it was fun to use photographs in a different medium.

Sally Fortner Memorial Quilt by Gayle Sacchetti, 1999, Cary, Illinois, 43" x 48".

This quilt is made in memory of Sally Fortner. Sally was part of our United Airlines family in Chicago for more than thirty years and lost her battle against breast cancer on January 12, 1999. It was Sally's wish that if we wanted to do something in her memory, we should raise funds for cancer research. This is how United Airlines became a sponsor for the American Cancer Society's Relay for Life team event in Barrington, Illinois.

The quilt started as a simple tribute to Sally, but grew into a fund-raiser as well. It includes six blocks filled with the signatures of her friends and co-workers, as well as signatures of cancer survivors. The Dazzling Star blocks were foundation pieced and used with the permission of designer Lisa Washburn. The entire quilt is machine pieced and machine quilted. It currently hangs in United Airlines' "Hall of Fame" in the Chicago sales office.

A Life Too Short by Lily G. Casura, 1999, Bellevue, Washington, 37" x 37".

In the summer of 1999, my dear friend Robin Bower passed away very young, leaving behind a loving family and many close friends. I wanted to do something special for Robin's mom, Mari Allen, to help keep Robin's memory alive. Photo transfer sounded like just the technique, and colorful batiks captured Robin's love for life and exuberant presence.

I borrowed the photos on the sly from her family, resized each one, and transferred them onto cotton and satin fabrics. My favorite photo (top row, middle) of a tiny, gleeful Robin in a galvanized washtub was resized from an ancient 2"-square Polaroid, and it enlarged very well. The overall design is a "cycle" of Robin's life, from childhood on. My husband helped me think through the challenging details: mitered corners and a continuous binding. I used gold metallic thread to hand quilt individual designs in the batiks. Robin's mom treasures this quilt and the memories it inspires.

Antique Trading-Card Quilt by Sue Van Gerpen, 2000, North Bend, Washington, 57" x 71". Machine quilted by Becky Kraus. Advertising trading cards collected by my great-grandmother Anna Sommers were the inspiration for this quilt. Anna and her girlfriend filled several scrapbooks with the cards during the late 1800s. As a child, I delighted in paging through the scrapbooks of advertising cards and memorabilia of an earlier time. As an adult, I still love to look at them!

Quilt for Baby Parker by Nancy Martin, 2000, Woodinville, Washington, 33" x 41".

The first-born child is always special, so I wanted to make a special quilt for my niece Colleen's expected baby. Wanting to match the décor of the nursery, I requested a color scheme and description. Colleen sent me samples of the wallpaper and border. Starting there, I cut 4½" animal-face squares from the wallpaper border. I transferred the squares to muslin and used them as the centers of the star blocks. The rest of the star blocks repeat the colors used in the room. Colleen, John, and baby Parker William Miele all love this bright and cheerful wall hanging.

Patrick's Portfolio by Margaret Sexton Moore, 2000, Seattle, Washington, 40" x 40". Machine quilted by Sue Lohse.

My son, Patrick, is a left-handed child who struggles with art projects from inception to completion. At the end of the first grade, he brought home a portfolio of artwork he had done throughout the year. I was overwhelmed as I sorted through the pieces, because I knew how difficult they had been for him to produce. I felt a need to honor Patrick's tremendous efforts, and the result is this quilt.

First Love by Diane O'Dell, 2000, Mountlake Terrace, Washington, 38" x 26".

This quilt was made with love for Tabith Jade (Tabi to me), by her grandma Diane and her mother, Cami, who took the pictures of Tabi at her riding lesson. We wanted to commemorate her love of horses in color, fabric, and design. As Tabi is an excellent artist, this photo quilt is doubly meaningful because it is made with her favorite colors. Tabi shares her love of horses with her good friend Sheryl, who also appears in the photos.

Riley's Halloween Quilt by Heather Fitzpatrick, 1999, Seattle, Washington, 69" x 81".

After being overwhelmingly inspired by Sandy's class, it took many hits and misses until I came up with this idea for my first original quilt design. The theme was a given from the start because Halloween is my son's favorite holiday. First sketched out on freezer paper, then transferred to graph paper, my quilt took shape as I experimented into the wee hours of many nights. I worked on it in secrecy, because I wanted it to be a surprise gift for Riley's fourth birthday. It hasn't received any ribbons, but it will always be a winner because it makes my son smile.

In Memory of Gwen by Sandy Bonsib, 1998, Issaquah, Washington, 20" x 29". Quilted by Becky Kraus.

When I met my husband more than twenty years ago, Gwen, his Labrador retriever, was his constant companion. He took this picture of her on a camping trip. She accompanied him everywhere, including his college classes. She was "Best Dog" in our wedding and continued to enjoy good health until our children were three and five years old. At the ripe old age of fourteen, Gwen peacefully died. Some years later, I read an article written about a faithful Lab and his adventures with the man he loved. Inspired by this piece, I wrote about Gwen, printed the text, and photo-transferred it to fabric, along with the picture, to create this quilt.

Fabric and Fotos by Janice Eggleston, 1999, Corinth, New York, 44" x 41".

This quilt combines two of my favorite hobbies, quilting and photography. It contains photos of my grandchildren and their pets, all taken over the past few years. I designed the setting, did some machine quilting on the photo transfers, and hand quilted the fabric around them. This quilt was my first attempt at a photo-transfer project, and I enjoyed the process and especially the results.

The Ties That Bind by Kathy Staley, 2000, Everett, Washington, 70" x 55".

This quilt combines history through photos and cloth. The forty-eight-star flag is made from linen, and the faded price, still on the back, says $5.50. The wool blanket is sixty years old and belonged to my grandparents. The photos are of my family and my husband's family, and they include several from the 1800s. I tried to go back as far as possible. The oldest photos I found, located in the top right corner, were of my great-great-great-grandparents. I thank my sister, Cindy, for encouraging me to make this quilt and for providing names and dates to help me piece our past.

Roxie's Laughter by Rosetta Greek, 2000, Seattle, Washington, 63" x 79". Machine quilted by Becky Kraus.

This quilt was made with love for my best friend, Roxanne Oliver. I wanted to make a quilt for her that represented the innocence and laughter of her youth. When Roxie was a little girl, she had two favorite things: her book *Queer, Dear Mrs. Goose* and her dog, Spot. Roxanne would read her book to Spot over and over again—there were times when Spot would be dressed in a T-shirt and underwear just for the occasion. Attentively, Spot would sit and listen to little Roxie recite the prose of her treasured book. Images from the book are used with permission from the author's family.

Gone Fishing by Charol Riedel, 2000, Port Orchard, Washington, 47" x 40".

I wanted to do something special for my husband's fiftieth birthday. Since he admired his father so much, a man who was taken from us too early, I decided I would give my husband a visual reminder of how special his father was to both of us. Making the quilt brought back a lot of good memories of my father-in-law. It was almost like having him there with me. This quilt hangs in a place of prominence in our home and gives my husband a chance to share memories of his dad with our friends.

Happy Seventieth Wedding Anniversary by Karen Galvin, 1999, Atlanta, Georgia, 49" x 26".

This quilt was designed as a gift to my grandparents, Waymond and Beatrice Totten, for their seventieth wedding anniversary. My grandparents have quilted all their lives, and through this art they passed on an incredible gift of family heritage. I wanted to create a piece that would include pictures from their lives together—a piece that would symbolize their unconditional love and loyalty.

My grandparents live on a farm in Yanceyville, North Carolina. Georgia Bonesteel, our quilting instructor, had the idea of incorporating an abstract outline of North Carolina, where my grandparents were born and raised, and where they nurtured generations of our family. I chose the "African Market Place" fabric as the backing and center of the quilt in order to highlight a rich family heritage and culture. In the center of the state is a small picture of my grandparents' farmhouse and the "rows" of fabrics emanating from the house represent the farm itself and its plentiful harvest. As my grandmother remarked, through photo transfers we have taken the art of quilting to a new level.

Fireplace Mantel by Kelly Kelsey, 1999, Gallatin Gateway, Montana, 143" x 18".

Every year I hold a quilt retreat at our ranch, the Nine Quarter Circle, in Gallatin Gateway, Montana, and last year Georgia Bonesteel came to teach. One of the classes she taught was on making photo-transfer quilts.

I used black-and-white photos that I had taken of my children. I knew I wanted to incorporate the photos in a fireplace mantel, but I needed to figure out how to frame them in a way that would show them off. I played with different shapes to put around them, and since we live on a ranch, the idea of a horseshoe seemed most appropriate. We all love the result, and it looked great on display at Christmas.

We've Grown by Ann Hanewald, 1999, Elmira, New York, 45" x 43".

This quilt was started in a class given by Georgia Bonesteel at the John C. Campbell Folk School. Since our four children are scattered all over the world—South Carolina, Tennessee, Germany, and El Salvador—I thought it appropriate that the photos follow the Trip Around the World pattern. The center section pictures my husband and me with our children, Matthew, Marta, Michael, and Megan. Each of the four corners is dedicated to one of the children and includes photos from infancy to marriage.

Days Gone By by Patricia DiTella, 2000, Barrington Hills, Illinois, 42" x 48". Machine quilted by Julie Christoffel.

I started out wanting to make a quilt for my husband, Phil. Both of his parents passed away recently and I thought a photo quilt commemorating their lives would be a special gift. I attended a quilting retreat with Georgia Bonesteel, who happened to be teaching classes on memory quilts. She recommended using Sandy Bonsib's *Quilting Your Memories* book to help with my project.

The pictures I chose were of varied sizes, which created a challenge. Since the photographs were old and mostly black-and-white, I selected reproduction fabrics to create an antique look. The photographs are all of my husband's family. They include his father in the middle and his mother at upper right. There are photos of her at a young age with her mother and father, as well as photos of my husband from infancy through his graduation from medical school. This will be a family heirloom and cherished for a long time.

From Sea to Shining Sea by Stephanie McCormick, 2000, Midland, Michigan, 39" x 49½".
This quilt started as a challenge in my local guild. The theme was Environment 2000. When I started looking through my photo albums for ideas, I discovered I had been to many places and that bodies of water attracted me most. The label on the back includes the names and places of these bodies of water. The challenge is to identify them without checking the label! I call this quilt *From Sea to Shining Sea,* although after all the problems I had with it, my sister suggested "Troubled Water" might be more appropriate.

God's Garden by Linda Thomas, 1999, Kirkland, Washington, 44" x 35".

After my father died last year, I decided to make a photo-transfer quilt in his memory for my mother. The title is from a poem used on the Mass card at his service. My mom sent two of Dad's favorite ties to use in the quilt. The appliquéd blocks are from Gabrielle Swain's book *From a Quilter's Garden.* I used Steam-A-Seam 2 to fuse the shapes to the background fabric. Various memories and comments were handwritten on the red fabric and next to many of the photos.

Making the Photo-Transfer Projects

Guidelines to remember as you make the projects in this book:

* Unless otherwise noted, trim photos on fabric to a scant ¼" seam allowance, not a full measured ¼". This ensures that a tiny sliver of background fabric won't show through if you don't sew with a perfect ¼" seam allowance or stitch a perfectly straight seam.

* Cut fabric strips across the width of the fabric unless otherwise indicated. "Cut lengthwise" means to cut parallel to the selvages of the fabric.

* Photo-transfer blocks will be stiffer than regular fabric, unless you're transferring directly to fabric (see page 9) with a fabric sheet. For this reason I press seams away from the photo-transfer blocks.

* To make assembling the units easier, pressing-direction arrows are provided when the placement of the seam allowance is important. Arrows are not provided if the pressing direction doesn't matter. In these cases, press the seam allowances the way you prefer. When joining blocks in horizontal rows, press the seam allowances in opposite directions from row to row.

* The cut sizes of side and corner triangles are larger than necessary. I prefer to trim a little fabric rather than not have enough.

* Cutting dimensions are provided for border strips; however, it's always a good idea to measure your quilt top before you cut and add borders.

* In some of the quilts, the binding is cut on the bias to show off a stripe or plaid, and yardage is given accordingly. If you prefer straight-grain binding, you won't need as much fabric.

* Photo-transfer blocks don't stretch. It's not possible to ease them if measurements don't match. Keep this in mind as you plan the size of your blocks.

* Pins can leave holes in photo-transfer blocks. Sometimes they'll close up when pressed, sometimes they won't. To be safe, pin close to photo-transfer blocks, but not in them.

* Handling sometimes causes the appearance of whitish creases on photo transfers. These are just wrinkles, and fortunately they will iron out. Refer to the manufacturer's instructions to see whether you can iron directly on the transfer itself.

* Whenever possible, evaluate your photo transfers, fabrics, and blocks on a vertical surface at least ten feet away. You'll make better design decisions when everything is the same distance from your eye.

* Use my quilts as patterns for *your* quilts. Although your photographs might be different shapes and sizes than my photographs were, you can use my

quilts as patterns. How? Choose the same number of photographs that I did, and adjust your photographs' sizes to match mine. For example, in *Best Friends: Peanut the Pygmy Goat and Eddie Rabbit* on page 69, you'll need nine 5½" square photographs. If you want to make a quilt like *Meow!* on page 58 with photos of your favorite cat, collect nine pictures of your cat, and reduce or enlarge, if necessary, the images to fit a 6" square (set on-point in this quilt). Then choose colors for your quilt based on the colors in your photographs, and choose fabric amounts based on my pattern guidelines.

If you want to make a particular quilt I've shown, but don't have the right number of photos, feel free to change the number needed. But if you do this, you'll need to also adjust the fabric requirements and the cutting directions.

❧ Fabric colors are indicated in the yardage requirements. These are the colors I chose because they worked with the photographs and images I had. Be sure to evaluate your own photos and images and make color and fabric choices based on them.

❧ Most important, make my designs your own. Feel free to add special, personal touches. The point is to use my ideas as guidelines, and then to make photo-transfer quilts that appeal to you. Your best quilts will be those that are uniquely your own.

Detail of *Days Gone By*. See full quilt on page 53.

Meow!

$\mathcal{I}$ love reds, but the colors in these copyright-free cats suggested bright and muted tones of pink and peach, which I found more challenging. I used a small-scale, yellow-and-white checked linen for the transfers, and pinks, peaches, and reds to coordinate with the cats for the sixteen-patch blocks. The fabric for the side and corner triangles is a muted pink plaid that coordinates well with the other fabrics, but I chose it after the other blocks were made. *Meow!* was machine quilted by Becky Kraus.

Finished Quilt Size: 32" x 32"

MATERIALS: 42"-WIDE FABRIC	CUTTING (MEASUREMENTS INCLUDE ¼" SEAM ALLOWANCES)
9 photos, no larger than 4" x 4"	
½ yd. linen for photo transfers	9 squares, each 6" x 6"
⅛ yd. each of 16 assorted pink, red, and peach prints for 16-Patch blocks	1 strip, 1⅞" x 42", from each of the 16 fabrics (16 strips total)
½ yd. plaid for setting triangles	4 squares, 10" x 10"; cut squares twice diagonally to yield 12 side triangles 2 squares, 6" x 6"; cut squares once diagonally to yield 4 corner triangles
1 yd. for backing	
¼ yd. for binding	4 strips, each 2" x 42"
4 yds. 1"-wide lace	
16 small buttons	

Directions

1. Transfer your images to transfer paper. Trim close to the edge of the transfers (⅛" away). Placing the image diagonally, center and press one image onto each 6" square of linen.

Trim close to the edge of each transfer.

2. Sew 4 different 1⅞" x 42" strips together to make a strip set. Repeat to make 3 more strip sets. Cut 16 segments, each 1⅞" wide, from each strip set. Sew 4 segments together, one from each strip set, to make a 16-Patch block. Make 16 blocks.

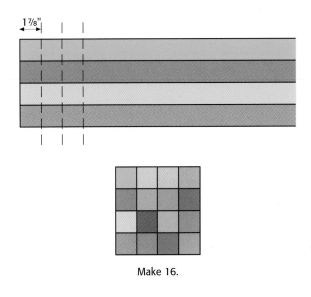

Make 16.

3. Arrange the photo-transfer blocks and 16-Patch blocks in diagonal rows. Rotate the 16-Patch blocks so the same fabric appears in different positions. Add the side triangles. Sew the blocks and side triangles into diagonal rows. Join the rows and add the corner triangles last.

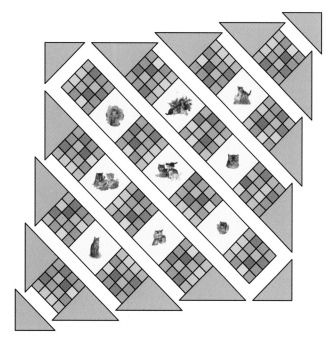

4. Align the ½" mark on the ruler with the block points and trim the edges of the quilt to ½" from these points.

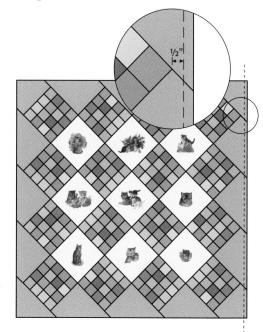

5. Layer your quilt with batting and backing; baste. Quilt as desired. Red thread was used for the quilting in the photo-transfer blocks to highlight the cats. Tan thread was used to quilt the rest of the quilt in various heart motifs.

6. On the back of the quilt, stitch lace to the edges, allowing ½" to show on the front. Add buttons referring to photo for placement.

7. Bind the edges, adding a sleeve if desired.

8. Add a label to your quilt.

My Baby Neville

$\mathcal{N}$eville is a yellow Labrador retriever puppy from the Guide Dogs for the Blind program. He was a part of our family for twelve months as we raised and trained him. Neville's picture is rich in tans, warm browns, and dark browns, colors that I carried through in my choice of fabrics. Note the quilting—dog paw prints in warm brown, bones in dark browns. This quilt features a single image sized 8" x 10". A 5" x 7" image would work, too, but you'd need to adjust the sizes of the rectangles and triangles that surround the photo. *My Baby Neville* was machine quilted by Becky Kraus.

Finished Quilt Size: 21" x 21"

MATERIALS: 42"-WIDE FABRIC	CUTTING (MEASUREMENTS INCLUDE ¼" SEAM ALLOWANCES)
1 photo, 8" x 10"	
⅓ yd. white solid for photo transfers	1 rectangle, 9" x 11"
¼ yd. light print or plaid for frame	2 rectangles, 2½" x 10½"
	2 rectangles, 2½" x 12½"
½ yd. medium print for inner triangles	2 squares, 13" x 13"; cut squares once diagonally to yield 4 triangles
½ yd. dark print for outer triangles	2 squares, 16" x 16"; cut squares once diagonally to yield 4 triangles
¾ yd. for backing	
⅓ yd. for binding	4 strips, 2" x 42"

Directions

1. Transfer your image to transfer paper. Center and press the photo onto the 9" x 11" rectangle of fabric. Trim the photo transfer to 8½" x 10½".

2. Sew the 2½" x 10½" rectangles to opposite sides of the photo transfer. Sew the 2½" x 12½" rectangles to the top and bottom edges.

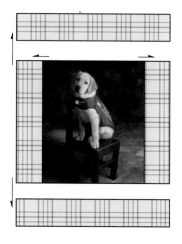

3. Fold the block in half on each side to find the midpoint; mark with a pin. Fold the inner triangles in half on the longest edge and mark the center with a pin. Matching the pins, sew a triangle to opposite sides of the photo-transfer block. Trim the excess fabric.

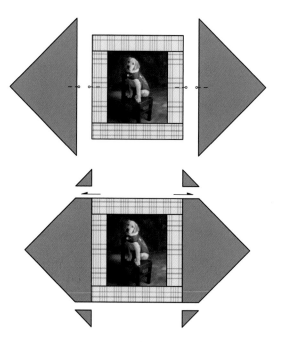

4. Matching the midpoints again, sew a triangle to the remaining sides of the block. Align the 1¼" mark on the ruler with the points of the frame and trim the edges to 1¼" from these points.

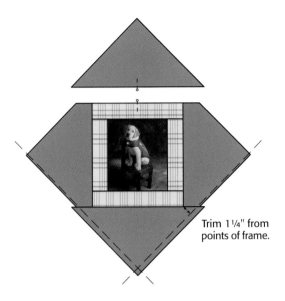

Trim 1¼" from points of frame.

5. Repeat steps 3 and 4 with the outer triangles. Align the ¼" mark on the ruler with the points of the inner triangles and trim the edges of the quilt to ¼" from these points.

6. Layer your quilt with batting and backing; baste. Quilt as desired. Dog prints were quilted in medium brown and dog bones were quilted in dark brown.

7. Bind the edges, adding a sleeve if desired.

8. Add a label to your quilt.

Creative Options

It's easy to make variations of this pattern. In *Our Family* (below) and *Dad's Family* (page 95), black triangles cover the corners of the photo-transfer blocks to give them an old-fashioned look. *Ben and Kate* includes a double frame, one narrow and one wide. The frame was eliminated altogether in *Julia* and the triangles were sewn directly to the sides of the photo-transfer block.

Our Family

Ben and Kate

Julia

By the Sea, By the Sea . . .

The rich blues, pinks and oranges of this quilt were inspired by the colors in the photographs. For the center of the quilt, I paired these colors with a soft tan. I made the borders large so I would have room for large photos. Before I appliquéd the photos to the quilt top, the border looked too wide. However, once I discovered a placement I liked, the borders weren't wide enough, so I added a second border in the same fabrics so that my goof would go unnoticed. I embellished the quilt with appliquéd lines and stars, representing wandering paths in the sand and sea stars in the water. The free-motion quilting was done by Becky Kraus.

Finished Quilt Size: 56½" x 64½"

MATERIALS: 42"-WIDE FABRIC	CUTTING (MEASUREMENTS INCLUDE ¼" SEAM ALLOWANCES)
6 images, 5" x 7" or 8" x 10"	
¾ yd. white solid for photo transfers	6 rectangles, 6" x 8", for 5" x 7" images or 6 rectangles, 9" x 11", for 8" x 10" images
½ yd. light tan to frame photos	6 strips, 1¼" x 42"
⅓ yd. each of 3 medium or dark blues, pinks, or oranges	2 strips, 2½" x 42" from each fabric (6 strips total) 2 strips, 3" x 42" from each fabric (6 strips total)
⅛ yd. *each* of 20 assorted blue, pink, and orange prints for Four Patch blocks	1 strip, 2½" x 21", from each of 20 fabrics (20 strips total)
2½ yds. tan #1 for Four Patch blocks and borders	20 strips, 2½" x 21", for Four Patch blocks 2 strips, 8½" x 40½", for inner side borders 2 strips, 8½" x 32½", for inner top and bottom borders 6 strips, 4½" x 42", for outer border
½ yd. tan #2 for corner squares	4 squares, 8½" x 8½", for inner border 4 squares, 4½" x 4½", for outer border
½ yd. blue solid for vine	Enough 1¼"-wide bias strips to yield 160" of bias strip when pieced together
¾ yd. total assorted fabrics for stars	3 of Template A 6 of Template B
3½ yds. for backing	
¾ yd. for bias binding	Enough 2"-wide bias strips to yield 250" of bias binding when pieced together

Directions

1. Transfer your images to transfer paper. Center and press one image onto each rectangle of fabric. Trim excess fabric, leaving only a scant ¼" seam allowance all around. Measure the length of the photo-transfer blocks. Cut 12 rectangles to this measurement from the 1¼"-wide strips. Sew the rectangles to opposite sides of each block. Measure the width of the block, including the strips just added. Cut 12 rectangles to this measurement from the remaining 1¼"-wide strips. Sew the rectangles to the top and bottom edges.

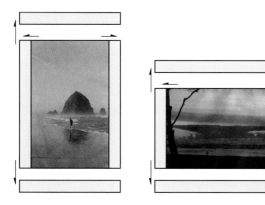

2. In a similar manner, measure and cut rectangles from the 2½"-wide strips for the sides of the photo-transfer blocks, and from the 3"-wide strips for the top and bottom edges. Set the blocks aside; they will be appliquéd to the quilt top later.

3. Sew a 2½" x 21" tan strip to each of the assorted 2½" x 21" strips. Cut 8 segments, each 2½" wide, from each strip set for a total of 160 segments. Sew 2 matching segments together, turning one of the segments, to make a Four Patch block. Make 80 blocks.

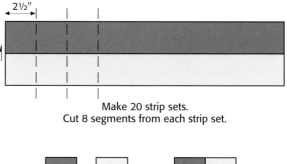

Make 20 strip sets.
Cut 8 segments from each strip set.

Make 80.

4. Arrange the Four Patch blocks as desired into 10 rows of 8 blocks each. Sew the blocks together in horizontal rows. Press the seams in alternate directions from row to row. Join the rows.

5. Sew the 8½" x 40½" border strips to opposite sides of the quilt top. Add the 8½" corner squares to the remaining 8½"-wide border strips, and sew these to the top and bottom edges.

6. Sew the six 4½"-wide strips together to make one long strip. From the long strip, cut 2 strips, 4½" x 56½", for side borders, and 2 strips, 4½" x 48½", for top and bottom borders. Sew the 56½"-long border strips to opposite sides of the quilt top. Add the 4½" corner squares to the remaining 4½"-wide border strips, and sew these to the top and bottom edges.

7. Arrange the photo-transfer blocks on the quilt top as desired, or see page 28 for placement options. Appliqué the blocks in place using your desired method. (I used needleturn appliqué.) Note that 2 blocks overlap the edge of the quilt onto the back. I did not appliqué the corners that would overlap the quilt edge until after the binding was complete.

8. Sew 1¼"-wide bias strips together to make one long strip. Fold the bias strip in half, wrong sides together, and stitch with a ⅛"-wide seam. Press the sewn strip, centering the seam on one side. Cut strips and arrange them as desired, seam sides down, to go between the appliquéd photos. Appliqué in place by hand or machine, turning under the edges that abut a block.

9. Arrange stars on quilt top and appliqué in place.

10. Layer your quilt with batting and backing; baste. Quilt as desired. My quilting features waves, sometimes overlapping like a turbulent sea.

11. Bind the edges, adding a sleeve if desired. Finish appliquéing any photographs that overlap the edges of the quilt.

12. Add a label to your quilt.

Quilting detail of *By the Sea, By the Sea . . .*

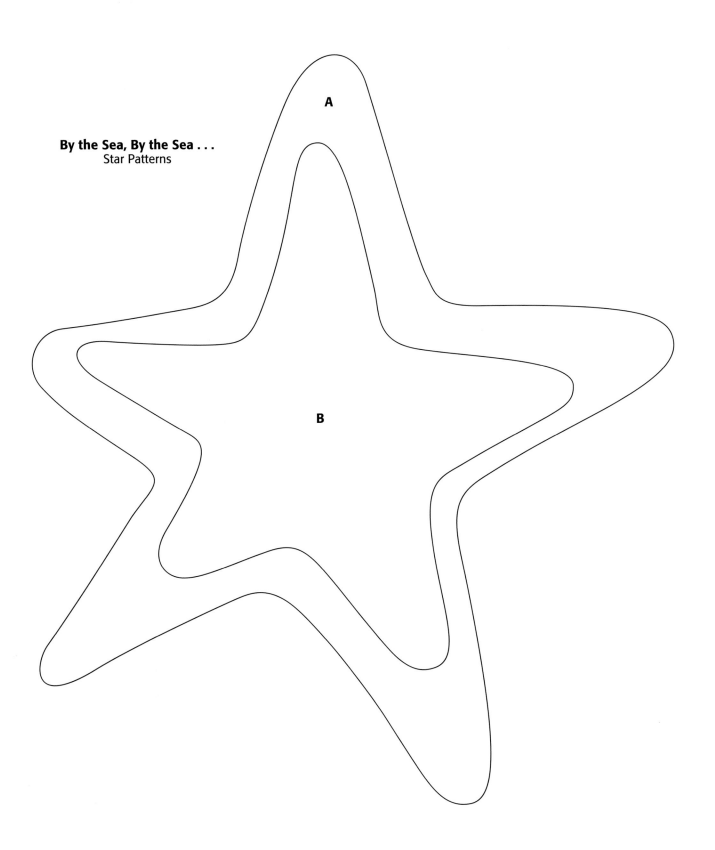

By the Sea, By the Sea . . .
Star Patterns

A

B

Best Friends: Peanut the Pygmy Goat and Eddie Rabbit

$\mathcal{T}$he grass is very green in these photographs, and I wanted to be sure that the fabrics I used emphasized the animals, not the grass. Initially I chose gold—to emphasize the rabbit—and blue—to emphasize the blue-gray color of the goat, but it really didn't work. As I experimented, I noticed that green's complement, red, actually calmed the bright green. I experimented further and finally chose a tan plaid frame to emphasize Eddie, blue-gray sashing to emphasize Peanut, and red cornerstones to calm the green and create a subtle chain between the blocks. The background white-and-tan print provides contrast for the on-point design and helps emphasize the white accents on Peanut's ears and nose. The lovely quilting was done by Becky Kraus.

Finished Quilt Size: 42½" x 42½"

MATERIALS: 42"-WIDE FABRIC	CUTTING (MEASUREMENTS INCLUDE ¼" SEAM ALLOWANCES)
9 photos, 5" x 5"	
½ yd. white for photo transfers	9 squares, 6" x 6"
½ yd. light plaid for frames	5 strips, 2" x 42"; crosscut strips into 36 rectangles, 2" x 5½"
⅓ yd. red print for cornerstones	4 strips, 2" x 42"; crosscut strips into 64 squares, 2" x 2", and 4 rectangles, 2" x 2½"
½ yd. gray print for sashing	5 strips, 2" x 42"; crosscut strips into 16 rectangles, 2" x 8½"; 4 rectangles, 2" x 5½"; and 4 rectangles, 2" x 2½"
1 yd. light print for background and borders	3 strips, 2" x 42"; crosscut strips into 8 squares, 2" x 2"; 8 rectangles, 2" x 3½"; and 8 rectangles, 2" x 5"
	3 strips, 6½" x 42"; crosscut strips into 4 rectangles, 6½" x 8½"; and 4 rectangles, 6½" x 14½"
	2 strips, 2" x 39½", for side borders
	2 strips, 2" x 42½", for top and bottom borders
2½ yds. for backing	
⅜ yd. for binding	5 strips, 2" x 42"

Directions

1. Transfer your images to transfer paper. Center and press one image onto each 6" square of fabric. Trim the photo transfers to 5½" x 5½".

2. Sew a 2" x 5½" rectangle to opposite sides of each photo transfer. Sew a 2" square to each end of the remaining 2" x 5½" rectangles. Sew these to the top and bottom of each photo transfer.

Make 9.

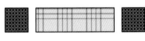

Make 18.

Make 9.

3. Sew 3 photo-transfer blocks and two 2" x 8½" sashing strips together to make each of 3 rows. Sew three 2" x 8½" sashing strips and two 2" squares together to make each of 2 sashing rows.

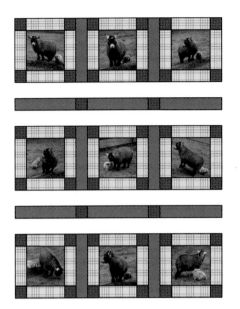

4. Sew the rows of blocks and rows of sashing together.

5. Sew the remaining squares and sashing pieces together to make the side blocks.

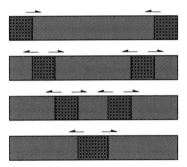

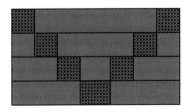

Make 4.

6. Sew a 6½" x 8½" rectangle to opposite sides of 2 of the side blocks. Sew these to the sides of the quilt. Sew a 6 ½" x 14½" rectangle to opposite sides of the remaining side blocks. Sew these to the top and bottom edges of the quilt.

7. Sew the 2" x 39½" border strips to opposite sides of the quilt. Sew the 2" x 42½" border strips to the top and bottom edges.

8. Layer your quilt with batting and backing; baste. Quilt as desired.

9. Bind the edges, adding a sleeve if desired.

10. Add a label to your quilt.

Quilted curves balance the quilt top's straight lines and echo the rounded shapes of Eddie and Peanut.

Cookie Jar

Chocolate-chip cookies are my favorite food, so it was easy to feature them in a quilt. The hardest part was getting good pictures of them! For fabrics, I chose numerous tones of brown, dark brown, and red that appeared in the cookies, as well as complementary blue-violet. The idea of placing the cookies in a cookie jar occurred to me at 5:30 one morning, so of course I had to get up and make it. The cookie recipe is stitched onto the back of the quilt. Machine quilted by Becky Kraus.

Finished Quilt Size: 39½" x 42"

MATERIALS: 42"-WIDE FABRIC	CUTTING (MEASUREMENTS INCLUDE ¼" SEAM ALLOWANCES)
9 images, about 4" x 4"	
½ yd. Osnaburg for photo transfers	9 squares, 7" x 7"
½ yd. tan solid #1 for inner frame	9 strips, 1¼" x 42"
½ yd. dark brown solid for outer frame	12 strips, 1" x 42"
⅛ yd. each of 15 assorted reds and browns for blocks, sashing, and border	2 strips, 2" x 42", from each of the 15 fabrics (30 strips total)
⅛ yd. violet print for accent, for blocks, sashing, and border	2 strips, 2" x 42"
¼ yd. tan solid #2 for jar lid	1 strip, 6" x 39½"
1⅓ yds. for backing	
½ yd. for binding	6 strips, 2" x 42"

Directions

1. Transfer your images for the blocks to transfer paper. Trim close to the edge of the transfers (⅛" away). Center and press one image onto each 7" square of Osnaburg.

2. Place Template A at each corner of the photo-transfer blocks and trim the corners to create an 8-sided block.

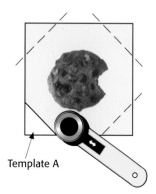

Template A

3. Starting on any side, sew a 1¼" tan solid #1 strip to the edge. Press the seam toward the frame and trim the excess even with the sides of the octagon. Working clockwise, sew a tan solid #1 strip to each side of the octagon, trimming after each strip is added.

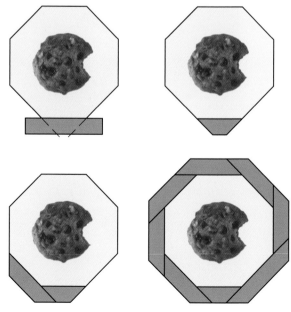

Make 9.

4. Repeat step 3 with a 1"-wide dark brown strip. Measuring through the centers, the blocks should be 9½" x 9½" (including seam allowances).

5. Select 9 of the 2" x 42" assorted strips and make 3 strips sets of 3 strips each. Cut 18 segments, 2" wide, from each strip set for a total of 54 segments. Sew 3 segments (one from each strip set) together to make a Nine Patch block. Make 18 blocks.

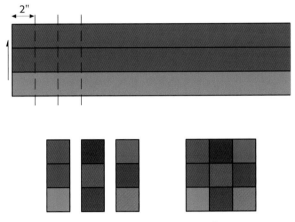

Make 18.

6. Using Template B, cut 2 triangles from each Nine Patch block. Sew a triangle to each corner of a photo-transfer block.

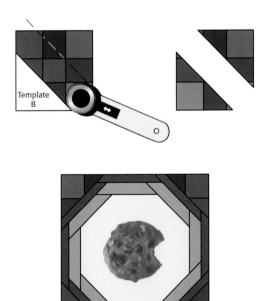

Make 9.

7. Sew 6 assorted 2" x 42" strips together to make a strip set. Repeat to make a second strip set with 6 fabrics. Make a third strip set with 7 assorted strips. Cut the strip sets into 2"-wide segments.

8. Arrange the photo-transfer blocks in 3 rows of 3 blocks each, leaving space between the blocks. Add the 6-square segments to the top of the blocks. Add the 7-square segments to the left side of each block, to the right of the blocks on the right side of the quilt, and at the bottom of the first 2 columns of blocks. Make one 8-square segment by removing 2 squares from one of the remaining 6-square segments and sewing them to another 6-square segment. Add this to the bottom of the block in the last column. Evaluate your arrangement. Move strips, if needed, until they look pleasing.

9. Sew the 6-square segments to the tops of the blocks. Sew the 7-square segments and blocks into horizontal rows. Sew the rows together.

10. Sew the segments at the bottom of the quilt together into one long strip and add this to the bottom of the quilt.

11. Place the remaining segments around the quilt top, end to end, to create 2 additional rows of squares on each side of the quilt and 1 additional row on the top and bottom. Move the strips around until you're pleased with the arrangement, adding or removing squares as needed. Use the remaining strips to cut additional squares if needed.

12. Sew the segments for the top and bottom edges together to make 2 rows of 22 squares each. Sew these to the top and bottom edges. Sew the segments for the sides together to make 4 rows of 24 squares each. Sew 2 rows of squares to each side of the quilt.

13. Transfer letters to fabric. To create the letters, I chose my favorite font on the computer, printed the words, enlarged them on a black-and-white copier, and transferred them to transfer paper on a color laser copier. Trim your letters a scant ⅛" from the edges. Press letters onto the 6" x 39½" tan solid #2 strip for the lid of the cookie jar. I cut and pressed each letter separately so I could control the spacing between them.

14. Use Template C to trim the top left and right corners of the quilt top. Use Template D to trim the bottom left and right corners. This creates the shape of a cookie jar.

15. Sew the lid of the cookie jar to the top of the quilt, matching the center of the quilt top with the center of the strip.

16. Layer your quilt with batting and backing; baste. Quilt as desired.

17. Bind the edges, adding a sleeve if desired.

18. Add a label to your quilt.

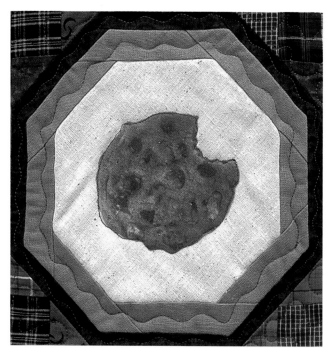

Detail from *Cookie Jar*

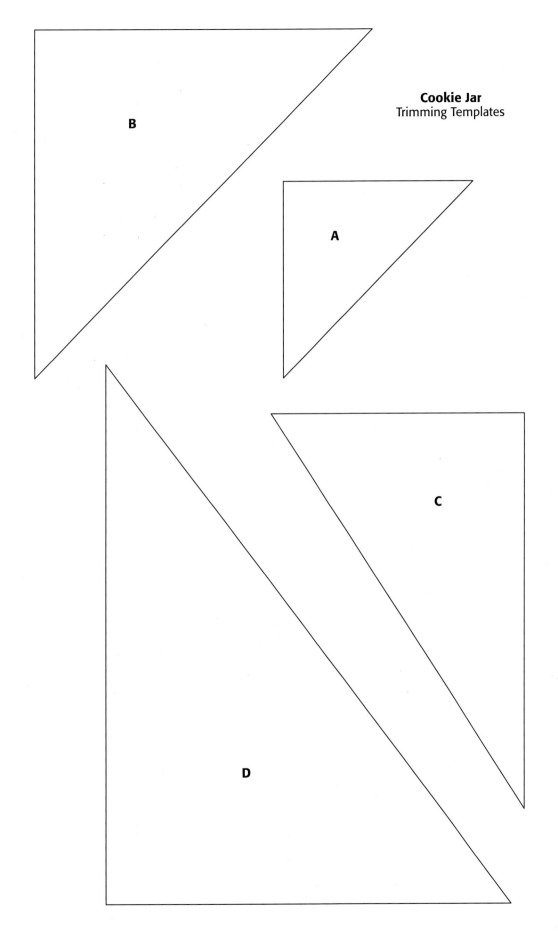

Cookie Jar
Trimming Templates

B

A

C

D

Mom's Quilt

*T*he photo in the center of this quilt is my favorite picture of my mother as a child. Because I don't have many good photos of her when she was young, I chose to add a picture of her and me taken when I was a baby. The subtle brown tone of these old photos suggested light brown and off-white fabrics. Also notice that when a photo is oval, you'll see more of the background fabric, so be sure to use a background fabric that coordinates well with the other fabrics in the quilt.

Because the photos are different sizes and because I wanted to place the photos in a step arrangement rather than in a row, I added small pieced hearts to balance the design. The rectangular photo was transferred onto an extra-large rectangle so I could trim it, leaving ½" of the background fabric showing. Although this wasn't necessary, I did it so that it would coordinate with the backgrounds of the two oval photos. Machine quilted by Becky Kraus.

Finished Quilt Size: 26" x 38"

MATERIALS: 42"-WIDE FABRIC	CUTTING
	(MEASUREMENTS INCLUDE ¼" SEAM ALLOWANCES)

3 photos:
     4½" x 5½" (Photo A, left)
     5" x 7½" (Photo B, middle)
     3½" x 5" (Photo C, right)	

¼ yd. white solid for photo transfers	6½" x 7½" (Photo A) 6½" x 9" (Photo B) 5½" x 7" (Photo C)
½ yd. ecru for heart blocks, background pieces, and inner border	2 squares, 2" x 2" 4 squares, 4" x 4"; cut squares once diagonally to yield 8 triangles 1 rectangle, 3" x 6½", for piece 1 2 rectangles, 1⅝" x 3½", for piece 2 1 rectangle, 2" x 6½", for piece 3 2 rectangles, 3¼" x 10½", for piece 4 2 rectangles, 2½" x 9", for piece 5 1 rectangle, 2" x 5½", for piece 6 2 rectangles, 1⅛" x 3½", for piece 7 1 rectangle, 3½" x 5½", for piece 8 2 strips, 2" x 14½", for piece 9 2 strips, 3½" x 14½", for side borders 2 strips, 2½" x 30½", for top and bottom borders
⅛ yd. *total* of 2 beige prints for heart blocks	6 squares, 2" x 2"
¼ yd. tan solid for middle border	2 strips, 1¼" x 18½", for side borders 2 strips, 1¼" x 30½", for top and bottom borders
¼ yd. *total* assorted medium tan prints for outer pieced border	16 squares, 4" x 4" for triangle units
¼ yd. *total* assorted light tan prints for outer pieced border	16 squares, 4" x 4", for triangle units 4 squares, 4½" x 4½", for corner blocks
¾ yd. for backing	
¼ yd. for binding	4 strips, 2" x 42"

Directions

1. Transfer your images to transfer paper. Center and press one image onto the matching background piece.

2. Using three 2" beige squares and one 2" background square, make a four-patch unit. Sew 2 background triangles to opposite sides of a four-patch unit. To center the triangles, align each triangle's point with the center seam in the unit. Trim the excess fabric.

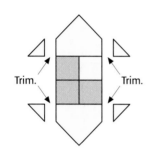

3. Sew a background triangle to the remaining sides of the four-patch unit. Trim the top and sides exactly at the points of the heart. Trim the bottom, leaving a ¼" seam allowance below the point of the heart.

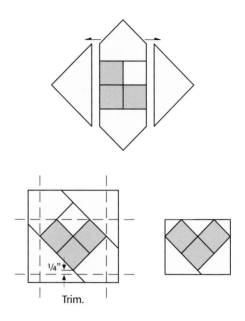

4. Referring to the illustration below, sew photo transfers, heart blocks, and background pieces together to make sections 1, 2, and 3. Sew the sections together, adding a piece 9 to each side.

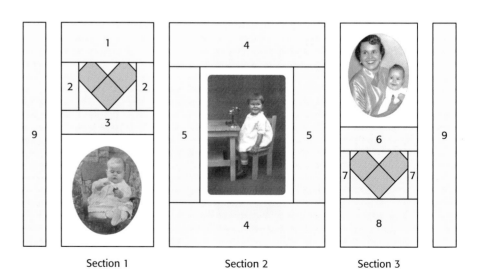

Section 1   Section 2   Section 3

80

5. Sew the 3½" x 14½" strips to opposite sides of the quilt top. Sew the 2½" x 30½" strips to the top and bottom edges.

6. Make half-square triangle units for the pieced borders. Draw a diagonal line on the wrong side of each 4" light square. Pair a 4" light and 4" medium square with right sides facing and the marked square on top. Stitch ¼" from both sides of the drawn line. Cut on the marked line. Trim the units to 3½" x 3½", using a Bias Square® ruler. Make 32 triangle units.

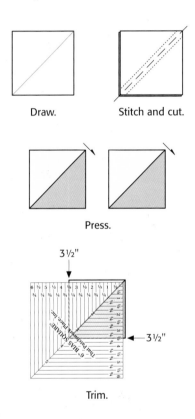

Draw. Stitch and cut.

Press.

Trim.

7. Referring to the illustration above right, sew 10 triangle units together to make each of the top and bottom borders. Sew 6 triangle units together to make each of the side borders. Be sure to orient the medium tan triangles toward the center of the quilt to create the zigzag pattern.

8. Sew the top pieced border to a 1¼" x 30½" middle border strip. Repeat for the bottom pieced border. Sew a side pieced border to a 1¼" x 18½" middle border strip. Repeat for the remaining side borders.

9. Sew the top and bottom borders to the top and bottom of the quilt top. Sew the 4¼" corner squares to each end of the side borders, and add these to the sides of the quilt.

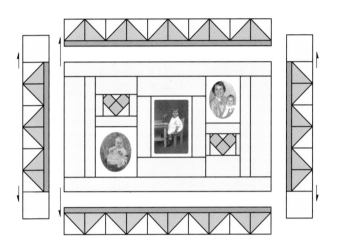

10. Layer your quilt with batting and backing; baste. Quilt as desired.

11. Bind the edges, adding a sleeve if desired.

12. Add a label to your quilt.

Wheat

$\mathcal{T}$he photo transfers for this quilt were created in an unusual way. I didn't start by taking a picture of the wheat. I laid the stalks of wheat directly on the copier glass. In fact, the black background in the images is really the underside of the copier lid! For the Log Cabin blocks, I chose many different gold fabrics to bring out the colors of the wheat. The outside border was a surprise. I expected this fabric to be too busy, but instead, I ended up liking it very much. Machine quilted by Becky Kraus.

Finished Quilt Size: 44½" x 49½"

MATERIALS: 42"-WIDE FABRIC	CUTTING (MEASUREMENTS INCLUDE ¼" SEAM ALLOWANCES)
4 images, 8" x 10½"	
½ yd. white fabric for photo transfers	4 rectangles, 11½" x 14"
⅛ yd. each of 24 assorted gold fabrics	1 strip, 1½" x 42", from each of the 24 fabrics (24 strips total)
⅜ yd. dark brown print	2 strips, 1½" x 38½", for inner side borders 2 strips, 1½" x 35½", for inner top and bottom borders 4 squares, 5" x 5", for corner squares 1 square, 2" x 2", for center diamond appliqué
⅔ yd. gold print	2 strips, each 5" x 40½", for outer side borders 2 strips, each 5" x 35½", for outer top and bottom borders
2¾ yd. for backing	
⅜ yd. for binding	5 strips, 2" x 42"

Directions

1. Transfer your images to transfer paper. Center and press one image onto each 11½" x 14" rectangle. Centering the image, trim the rectangle to 11" x 13½". This allows 1¼" of white background fabric to show on all 4 edges of the image, creating a built-in border.

2. Using a photo transfer as the center of the Log Cabin block, sew the first 1½"-wide strip to the right-hand side. Press, and trim excess fabric. Add a second strip to the bottom, using the same fabric. Press and trim.

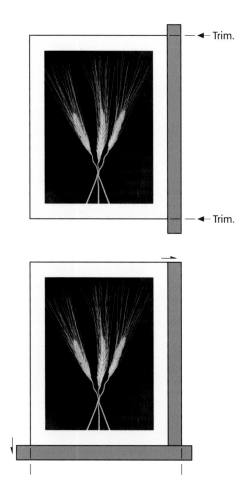

3. Select a second 1½"-wide fabric strip and sew it to the left side of the photo transfer. Press and trim. Sew the same fabric strip to the top. Press and trim.

4. Continue adding strips in this manner, using matching fabric on 2 adjacent sides of the block. Add strips until you have 3 strips on all sides of the photo transfer. Use 6 different 1½"-wide strips for each block. Make 4 Log Cabin blocks. Your blocks should be 17" x 19½" including seam allowances.

   Note: I arranged the gold fabrics in such a way that the darker ones met in the center of the quilt when I joined the four blocks.

Make 4.

5. Arrange the blocks into 2 rows of 2 blocks each. Sew the blocks together in horizontal rows, pressing seams to the right in the first row and to the left in the second row. Join the rows.

6. Sew the 1½" x 38½" dark brown strips to opposite sides of the quilt top. Press the seams toward the inner border strips. Sew the 1½" x 35½" dark brown strips to the top and bottom edges. Press.

7. Sew the 5" x 40½" outer border strips to opposite sides of the quilt top. Press the seams toward the outer border strips. Sew a 5" corner square to each end of the 5" x 35½" outer border strips and sew these to the top and bottom edges. Press.

8. Turn under a ¼" seam allowance all around the 2" dark brown square; press. Place this square on point in the center of the quilt, and stitch in place.

9. Layer your quilt with batting and backing; baste. Quilt as desired.

10. Bind the edges, adding a sleeve if desired.

11. Add a label to your quilt.

Detail of *Wheat's* border quilting

A Quilt of My Quilts

Many quilters take pictures of their quilts before giving them as gifts or using them. These photos represent a wonderful record of our creations. I thought I would go one step further and make a quilt about my favorite quilts! Because the quilts I photographed for this project were all different colors, it was a challenge to create a quilt that worked with all the rich colors that I love and yet still make sure that the photos were the stars of the quilt. I chose to make the photos the lightest areas in this quilt, and that's why they're not overwhelmed by the more colorful fabrics. Machine quilted by Becky Kraus.

Finished Quilt Size: 54" x 54"

MATERIALS: 42"-WIDE FABRIC	CUTTING (MEASUREMENTS INCLUDE ¼" SEAM ALLOWANCES)
13 photos, no larger than 8" x 8"	
1⅛ yd. white solid cotton	13 squares, 9" x 9"
⅓ yd. each of 13 assorted blues for background triangles	2 squares, 8½" x 8½", from each of the 13 fabrics (total 26 squares); cut squares once diagonally to yield 52 triangles
¾ yd. red for sashing	36 rectangles, 1¾" x 11"
1¼ yd. blue plaid for sashing posts and setting triangles	24 squares, 1¾" x 1¾", for sashing posts 2 squares, 19½" x 19½"; cut squares twice diagonally to yield 8 side triangles 2 squares, 13½" x 13½"; cut squares once diagonally to yield 4 corner triangles
3⅜ yd. for backing	
½ yd. for binding	6 strips, 2" x 42"

Directions

1. Transfer your images to transfer paper. Center and press one image onto each 9" square of fabric. Trim to a scant ¼" seam allowance around image. Your photo-transfer blocks may be different sizes, and that's OK.

2. Using 4 matching blue triangles for each photo, arrange the blocks and triangles until you're pleased with the combinations.

3. Sew 2 matching triangles to opposite sides of a photo-transfer block. Trim excess fabric. To center the triangles, fold the triangles and the photo-transfer blocks in half and mark the centers with pins.

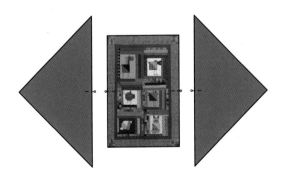

4. Add the 2 remaining matching triangles to the top and bottom of the photo-transfer block.

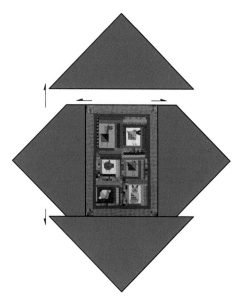

5. Trim each block to 11" x 11", centering the photo transfer.

6. Arrange the blocks, sashing strips, sashing posts, and side triangles in diagonal rows. Play with the arrangement of the blocks until you're satisfied. Sew the blocks and sashing strips into diagonal rows. Sew the sashing strips and sashing posts into diagonal rows. Join the rows and add corner triangles last.

7. Align the 1¼" mark on the ruler with the points of the sashing posts and trim the edges of the quilt to 1¼" from these points.

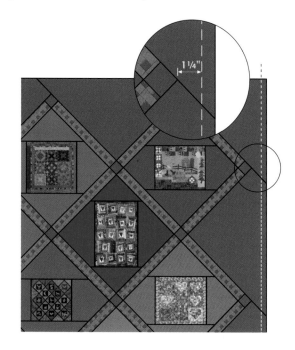

8. Layer your quilt with batting and backing; baste. Quilt as desired.

9. Bind the edges, adding a sleeve if desired.

10. Add a label to your quilt.

Falling Leaves

$\mathcal{T}$he photo-transferred leaves in this quilt were created from a single fake, but very colorful, leaf! I laid the leaf directly on the color copier's glass. The large leaf is shown at its original size, while the smaller leaves are a 40 percent reduction of the original. I decided to use blue and green fabrics for the half-square triangle units surrounding the leaves because the colors are complementary (opposite on the color wheel) to the colors in the leaves. Once I'd added the purple inner border, I had planned to add an outer green border to all four sides. However, when I glanced at the quilt with just the green top and bottom borders, I liked what I saw and decided to finish the quilt without adding the green side borders. Machine quilted by Becky Kraus.

Finished Quilt Size: 40" x 47"

MATERIALS: 42"-WIDE FABRIC	CUTTING (MEASUREMENTS INCLUDE ¼" SEAM ALLOWANCES)
12 images: three 7" x 7"; nine 3" x 3"	
½ yd. ecru solid	2 rectangles, 4½" x 12½" 3 squares, 4½" x 4½" 3 squares, 8½" x 8½"
26 squares of assorted green and blue-green prints in medium and dark values	each square 5⅛" x 5⅛"
26 squares of assorted blue and blue-violet prints in medium and dark values	each square 5⅛" x 5⅛"
⅜ yd. purple print	2 strips, 2¼" x 32½", for inner side borders 2 strips, 2¼" x 40", for inner top and bottom borders
½ yd. green print	2 strips, 6" x 40", for top and bottom outer borders
1½ yd. for backing	
⅜ yd. for binding	5 strips, 2" x 42"

The variation in scale of photo-transfer leaf images is highlighted in this detail of *Falling Leaves* quilt.

Directions

1. Transfer your images to transfer paper. Trim close to the edge of the transfers (⅛" away). Center and press one image onto each of the large and small squares. Center and press 3 images in a vertical row on one of the 12½" rectangles, and 3 images in a horizontal row on the remaining 12½" rectangle.

2. For half-square triangle units, pair a green or blue-green square with a blue or blue-violet square, right sides together. Mark a diagonal line on the back of the lighter square. Sew ¼" from both sides of the drawn line. Cut on the drawn line. Press the seams toward the dark fabric. Trim the units to 4½" x 4½", using a Bias Square ruler. Make 52 triangle units.

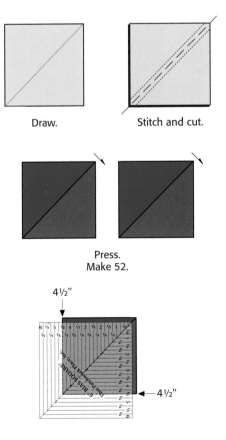

Draw.　　Stitch and cut.

Press.
Make 52.

4½"

4½"

3. Referring to the photo on page 89, arrange the photo-transfer blocks and triangle units until you have a pleasing arrangement. Sew the photo-transfer blocks and triangle units together in rows or sections as needed. Join the rows and sections.

4. Sew the 2¼" x 32½" inner border strips to opposite sides of the quilt top. Press the seams toward the inner borders. Sew the 2¼" x 40" inner border strips to the top and bottom edges. Press.

5. Sew the 6" x 40" outer border strips to the top and bottom of the quilt. Press the seams toward the outer borders.

6. Layer your quilt with batting and backing; baste. Quilt as desired.

7. Bind the edges, adding a sleeve if desired.

8. Add a label to your quilt.

Three Generations

$\mathcal{F}$or this quilt, I selected three photographs featuring three generations of the Bickley family: my husband, John Bickley, my children, Ben and Kate Bickley, and my mother-in-law, Dee Bickley. To make the photo-transfer blocks look as much like the original photographs as possible, I transferred the photographs onto very tightly woven satin. Because so many quilters love stars, I made Star blocks and arranged them in a vertical row. Machine quilted by Becky Kraus.

Finished Quilt Size: 30½" x 56½"

Materials: 42"-wide fabric	Cutting
	(Measurements include ¼" seam allowances)
3 photos, 4½" x 6½"	
¼ yd. white satin for photo transfer	3 rectangles, 7" x 9"
¼ yd. *each* of 3 different brown fabrics for Star blocks	From *each* brown fabric, cut: 1 square, 2⅞" x 2⅞"; cut square once diagonally to yield 2 triangles (A) 1 square, 3¼" x 3¼"; cut square twice diagonally to yield 4 triangles. You'll only use 2. 8 squares, 3" x 3", for triangle units (B) 2 rectangles, 2½" x 8½"
⅝ yd. of white fabric for Star blocks, sashing, and inner border	2 squares, 3¼" x 3¼"; cut squares twice diagonally to yield 8 triangles (B) for Star blocks. You'll only use 6. 24 squares, 3" x 3", for triangle units in Star blocks 12 squares, 2½" x 2½", for Star blocks 2 rectangles, 2½" x 14½", for sashing 2 strips, 2½" x 40½", for side borders 2 strips, 2½" x 18½", for top and bottom borders
1⅛ yd. floral for outer border	3 strips, 6½" x 42", for side borders 2 strips, 6½" x 30½", for top and bottom borders
1¾ yds. for backing	
⅜ yd. for binding	5 strips, 2" x 42"

Directions

1. Transfer your photos to transfer paper. Center and press one image on each 7" x 9" rectangle. Centering the photo, trim the photo-transfer blocks to 6½" x 8½".

2. Draw a diagonal line on the wrong side of the 3" white squares. Pair a white square with a 3" brown square. Sew ¼" from both sides of the drawn line. Cut on the drawn line. Trim the units to 2½" x 2½", using a Bias Square ruler. Make 16 matching half-square triangle units for each Star block.

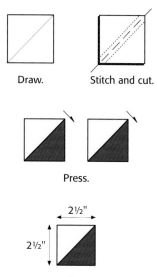

Draw.   Stitch and cut.

Press.

Make 16.

3. Sew a small white triangle (B), a small brown triangle (B), and a large brown triangle (A) together to make a quarter-square triangle unit. Make 2 units for each block.

Make 2
for each block.

4. Sew the units and the 2½" white squares together to make horizontal and vertical rows as shown. Sew a brown rectangle to opposite sides of the photo-transfer block. Sew a vertical row to opposite sides of the block. Sew the horizontal rows to the top and bottom edges of the block. Make 2 more Star blocks, using the other 2 brown prints.

Make 3.

5. Join the Star blocks in a vertical row with 2½" and 14½" sashing strips between the blocks.

6. Sew the 2½" x 40½" inner border strips to opposite sides of the quilt top. Sew the 2½" x 18½" inner border strips to the top and bottom edges.

7. Join the three 6½" x 42" outer border strips together to make one long strip. From the long strip cut 2 strips, 6½" x 44½" long. Sew these to opposite sides of the quilt top. Sew the remaining 6½" x 30½" outer border strips to the top and bottom edges.

8. Layer your quilt with batting and backing; baste. Quilt as desired.

9. Bind the edges, adding a sleeve if desired.

10. Add a label to your quilt.

Resources

IN THE BEGINNING FABRICS

8201 Lake City Way

Seattle, Washington 98115

206-523-8862

www.inthebeginningfabrics.com

Quilt Wall

THE LAP QUILTER

PO Box 96

Flat Rock, North Carolina 28731

www.georgiabonesteel.com

Grid Grip

MARTINGALE & COMPANY

PO Box 118

Bothell, WA 98041-0118 USA

800-426-3126

www.patchwork.com

Photo-transfer paper

Dad's Family by Sandy Bonsib. See "Creative Options" on page 63.

About the Author

*S*andy Bonsib is a teacher by profession, and a quilter by passion. She has a graduate degree in education, and has taught locally at the Seattle quilt shop In the Beginning since 1993, and nationally since 1997. She is the author of two books, *Folk Art Quilts: A Fresh Look* (Martingale & Company, 1998) and *Quilting Your Memories: Inspirations for Designing with Image Transfers* (Martingale & Company, 1999). Sandy has had quilts published in numerous magazines, most frequently *American Patchwork and Quilting*. She has also appeared on television, in *Lap Quilting with Georgia Bonesteel* (1999) and *Simply Quilts* with Alex Anderson (2000 and 2001). She was one of six featured artists on *Quilts of the Northwest* (PBS-KCTS9 in Seattle, 1998).

In addition to her quiltmaking and teaching, Sandy coordinates a group that makes quilts for the children of battered women, through In the Beginning Fabrics. For the past three years, she has also been a mentor for high school students working on their senior projects in quiltmaking. Sandy lives on Cougar Mountain in Issaquah, Washington, on a small farm with her husband, John, their two teenagers, Ben and Kate, and many animals. She is also a puppy raiser for Guide Dogs for the Blind.

For information on Sandy's classes and lectures, please contact:

Patchwork Northwest

Fax: 425-644-1392

E-mail: sjbonsib@aol.com